DEAR COACH

ADVANCE PRAISE

"Oftentimes, the last voices to be heard in sports are the most import-ant voices of all: the athletes. *Dear Coach* has given a voice to those athletes and provides a great reminder for coaches of every age and ability to take a moment, really listen, and provide the type of experience our athletes are craving."

—John O'Sullivan,
Author of *Every Moment Matters* and *Changing the Game,*
Founder of Changing the Game Project

"Prepare to be made relationally vulnerable! Every letter in this book made me wonder if I had actually written it to one of my old coaches, or if it could have been written by one of my former athletes to me. Dr. Erdner took me through my coaching emotions from start to finish and made me confirm that my *why* matches my *how*. As a sport leader, she challenged me to make sure our organization is truly taking care of our coaches emotionally and not just teaching x's and o's."

—Kevin Greene,
Director of Coach & Athlete Development at US Lacrosse

"*Dear Coach* is unlike any other book in the coaching field that I've seen. In fact, I'll call it groundbreaking for giving athletes the opportunity to respond to coaches in a way that allows them to be more open and honest than a typical coach/athlete end-of-season meeting might allow. I feel that all coaches—even those who are self-aware and reflective—would benefit from hearing what athletes had to say in a format such as this book. *Dear Coach* gives you a look at the actual good, the not-so good, and the truth (as Dr. Erdner calls it) that is the athlete/coach relationship in American sports. I highly recommend that no matter what your background may be or where you are in your coaching journey, you make this book a part of your library."

—Scott Caulfield, MA, CSCS*D, RSCC*D,
Director of Strength and Conditioning at Colorado College

"When Dr. Erdner and I first met, she was talking about this book she was writing, and from the outset I was intrigued by the passion with which she spoke of this book. If you are committed to being better at your craft, then this book is for you! It's for athletes, coaches, those who support coaches, and especially those who are lifelong learners. I agree with Dr. Erdner: everyone has a Dear Coach letter in them, and I bet, like me, you will write that letter after reading this book."

—Cameron Kiosoglous, PhD,
Director of the MS in Sport Coaching Leadership program at
Drexel University, US Rowing national team coach

"Dr. Erdner has given the world a book that coaches have always needed. What athletes have been too afraid to say to those in charge is now on paper for the world to see. It is a book that will shape the way you approach relationships with athletes with every single page!"

—Amanda Jones,
Assistant volleyball coach at West Florida University

DEAR COACH

What I Wish I Could Have Told You,

Letters from Your
ATHLETES

Sara Erdner | PhD, CMPC

NEW YORK

LONDON • NASHVILLE • MELBOURNE • VANCOUVER

Dear Coach

What I Wish I Could Have Told You, Letters from Your Athletes

Published in New York, New York, by Morgan James Publishing. Morgan James is a trademark of Morgan James, LLC. www.MorganJamesPublishing.com

ISBN 9781631952845 paperback
ISBN 9781631952852 eBook
Library of Congress Control Number: 2020942960

Cover & Interior Design by:
Christopher Kirk
www.GFSstudio.com

Morgan James is a proud partner of Habitat for Humanity Peninsula and Greater Williamsburg. Partners in building since 2006.

Get involved today! Visit
MorganJamesPublishing.com/giving-back

For those whose voices have been unheard

TABLE OF CONTENTS

INTRODUCTION

Dear Coach,

This book started brewing years ago when I was an athlete. I remember our smelly locker room after a day of major sweat, joining the rest of my teammates as we complained about our coaches:

- "She's just so UGHHHHH!"
- "Why would he have us do *that* drill when we need to work on *this*?"
- "It would be nice if she would acknowledge the work I've put in instead of only tearing me down."
- "Is he trying to kill us?"
- "He keeps acting like we're a family, but he doesn't even know me."

Practice after practice, game after game, we'd walk away from the coaches complaining. The next day, we'd greet them with a smile on our faces. Resentment grew as our disdain went unnoticed, which we passively communicated through our body language. This cycle of complain-smile-complain repeated itself year after year throughout the majority of my athletic career.

Looking back, it's no surprise that nothing ever changed in my twelve-plus years of competitive sport. Complaining is the equivalent of sitting in a rocking chair: you go nowhere. While I believe a certain amount of complaining can be cathartic, it reaches a point when it becomes detrimental. Thus, I began to wonder: What did I need from the coaches? Were my needs the same as other athletes? Why didn't we say anything?

As much as my ego hates to admit it, I didn't say anything to my coaches because I was scared. I was afraid to lose playing time and worried the coaches wouldn't like me. I was scared to ruffle feathers because I didn't want my teammates mad at me for pissing the coaches off, which would result in an astronomical number of sprints. All of this made me anxious to confront the coaches because I needed my teammates' friendships. It was a hard situation to navigate.

I weighed the pros and cons of telling our coaches everything we complained about, but after multiple days of biting my nails while I catastrophized every possible situation, the cons outweighed the pros. Every. Single. Time.

The passive act of complaining kept me, and the rest of my teammates, safe from the unknown: the coaches' reactions. In my mind, their reactions would most likely be negative, so I couldn't risk it. Plus, my teammates' friendships meant more to me at the time, so I couldn't risk their disapproval.

Now, I realize that, as an athlete, I didn't exactly know what I needed from the coaches—and I also didn't know how to articulate whatever those needs were. I was a developing young adult at the time who was still learning how to navigate my emotions, so how could I sit down with adults and discuss my needs in an emotionally mature way?

So, I never said anything. And this allowed pent-up emotions to undermine my performance. The less I talked to the coaches about my concerns, the more I lost respect for them. I know it sounds silly, but I lost respect because they weren't mind readers.

In an ideal world, it would have been nice if they had asked what I thought because all responsibility to mend the relationship should never fall on the athlete.

As I lost respect, I lost trust in their abilities to coach. So, when they would call a play during a high-stakes game, my first reaction was doubt, questioning whether that play was best at that moment. That split-second hesitation could've been the difference between winning and losing that particular possession. The coaches could have avoided that moment of doubt with good communication; good communication is what robbed us all of the potential to achieve greater things in sport.

As I resentfully retired from sport due to injury and transitioned to life as an undergraduate student, I had to choose a major. I chose a degree in communication studies from the University of Alabama-Huntsville (my hometown university) because I genuinely wanted to know more about the subject; maybe then I could understand my lived athletic experiences.

Once I got into my major courses, I was surprised by how much I enjoyed my undergraduate experience. So much so, I decided to pursue a communication studies master's degree from the University of Tennessee-Knoxville (UTK). As I delved deeper into my coursework at UTK, I became more intrigued with the interpersonal facet of communication, the nuances that determine how we navigate relationships effectively. As my fascination with interpersonal communication increased, I saw how these intricacies played out in the relationships with my former coaches.

My first theoretical love during my studies was uncertainty reduction theory[1] (URT). In a nutshell, this theory states that the relationship quality strengthens as uncertainty is reduced. Berger, the theoretical mastermind behind URT, says uncertainty is an uncomfortable feeling for most. Thus, we try to reduce it by, to note one of the theory's axioms, seeking information to get on the same page as the other.

My former coach-athlete relationships were starting to make more sense. One barrier in communication formed because we were not actively trying to get on the same page, probably because that's not the culture of sport, so we never really learned how. After all, in sport it is an unwritten rule that athletes are supposed to follow the lead of the coach without question. So, I experienced high uncertainty because seeking information from the coach did not seem allowed; I often was told I "should have been listening in the first place."

I was magically just supposed to *be* on the same page, which was always confusing when my coach communicated a different page, often within the confines of a few minutes. For example, I remember one situation where the coach scolded me for "not following the play like we executed in practice," and moments later demanded that I "get more creative with the play so we can keep the competition on their toes." This unwritten rule of unquestioning deference is what muddled my mind and resulted in a stalemate of my performance.

I needed to know more, so I registered for a sport psychology class in hopes I would find more information to understand this barrier in communication. I not only found that; I also discovered a world that changed the trajectory of my research, and my life, for the better.

Dr. Rebecca (Becky) Zakrajsek was the professor for my KNS 533: Psychology of Sport course at UTK. She also served as a committee member for my master's thesis, which examined the influence of parent communication patterns on student-athlete self-efficacy.[2] So, while I took her course, we often talked about our similar passions for communication, interpersonal relationships, and how they operate within sport. After creating a quality working relationship, Becky suggested for me to apply to be a PhD student under her mentorship. A year later, I became her new PhD student with the agreement that we would focus on researching various sport relationships. I was stoked. I had found some of the answers to my inquiry, but I still questioned the following:

1. What did I wish I had told my coaches but never did?
2. Were these the same things other athletes wished they could tell their coaches?
3. Why did we, the athletes, not tell our coaches these things?

I spoke with Becky about these questions. She was intrigued as well but also challenged me to lean into the sport psychology research. That is, I had to do what every PhD student must: read tons of research to determine how to fill in the gaps.

After a year of reading what felt like was the equivalent of five million five-hundred-page books, I became enamored with resilience in sport. At the time, it was a hot topic that not only demonstrated a high correlation with athlete well-being and performance but also credited athlete social support (e.g., the coach) as a vital factor in nurturing athlete resilience. Thus, I wanted to know more about the coach's role in building athlete resilience; however, I knew I needed to fill the gap. At the same time that I stumbled upon resilience in sport, I also was introduced to my second theoretical love: relational-cultural theory (RCT).[3] RCT theorists claim that all psychological growth happens in relationships, in quality connection with others. The moment that quality connection is broken, possibly due to a barrier in communication created by the interplay of various sociocultural factors and power dynamics,[4] psycholog-

xvi | **DEAR COACH**

ical distress occurs. That was the gap: I was going to explore the coach's influence on athlete resilience through the lens of RCT, which I secretly hoped would lead me to answers for why there was a lack of honest communication between player and coach.

I started by interviewing NCAA coaches. My overarching research question: How do coaches perceive they influence student-athletes' abilities to bounce back after major stress? The coaches provided many insights, but surprisingly the one resounding theme was their hunger to know what athletes thought about their coaching style. For the most part, every coach I interviewed made a statement similar to the following: "You know, Sara, it's all fine and well what we think, but you should be asking the athletes what they think about us. How are we doing? That's what I really want to know."

Honestly, I also was curious to know athletes' opinions on coaches' impact. It's what I wanted to know all along: What do athletes have to say? And is it the same or different than how I felt during my athletic years?

So I did what any good researcher is supposed to do first: I searched for existing research regarding athletes' perceptions of how their coach influenced their resilience. While I found a plethora of research by Drs. Mustafa Sarkar,[5] David Fletcher,[6] and colleagues[7] regarding what resilience is and how it operates in sport, I found no articles, at the time, that explored athletes' thoughts about coach impact on athlete resilience.

Then, I did the second most crucial thing any researcher would have done. After searching through scholarly journals and not being satisfied, I went to the bookstores: Barnes & Noble, Books-A-Million, Amazon. That is when I realized the problem was more profound.

What I saw in my initial exploration were books predominantly written by coaches: Pat Summit, John Wooden, Jen Welter, Urban Meyer, and Phil Jackson, to name a few. These coaches wrote about how they did it, how they led with heart to get athletes to perform and win. I also saw a few elite athletes' autobiographies, which gave a nod to their respective coaches for their winnings. What I didn't see, though, were books written by athletes to coaches addressing their wants and needs. I must admit, I wasn't surprised. Across the years, what I gathered from my own experience as well as through observation of others was that athletes don't feel safe to express themselves to their coaches; thus, they wouldn't dare question the system. The system begets the system, which perpetuates the cycle of coaches neglecting athlete stories. So, why would athletes waste their energy writing a book about it?

As mentioned, coaches craved to know what athletes thought. While I found research that privileged athletes' voices (research that the general public cannot freely or easily access), I only found silence on the bookshelves available to the consumer. That's when I realized I would not find my groundbreaking answers only by interviewing coaches. From the looks of those bookshelves, we've already heard everything we need to hear from them. It was high time to hear from the athletes. I believed they held the keys to move sport forward in a better, more efficient direction. That is why, for my dissertation, I turned my attention to athletes. I wanted to know how *they* felt their coaches influenced them when they experienced major stress.

What I anticipated being standard sixty- to ninety-minute interviews with athletes ended up being heart-rendering two-and-a-half to three-hour-long cathartic conversations. Why? Because this was the first instance during which these athletes had a platform—

other than complaining to their teammates—to discuss how their coach influenced them on a deep level. After hearing what they had to say, I knew it would be a disservice to keep their stories locked away in some research publication. Thus, I decided to write this book after completing my dissertation thereby bringing my research highlighting athletes' voices to your bus ride, coffee shop talk, and leisure reading before bed. Looking at those bookshelves, I saw a gap. After sitting down with athletes and listening to them, I became more and more confident their stories are what we *need* to fill the void.

Why? Because in my interviews with athletes, they spilled everything. Their frustrations. Their gratitude. Their trials. Their triumphs. Tears were shed. Chills were shared. I asked why they didn't share their stories with their coaches. Their answers were insightful. Every athlete I encountered did not share their stories because of—no surprise to me—barriers in communication due to dysfunctional power dynamics within the coach-athlete relationship. This finding fueled my new mission: dissolving this barrier.

After successfully defending my dissertation, I turned my attention toward creating a solution I believed would more quickly reach and positively influence the masses. I started by pitching the idea of this book to a few athletes who expressed interest in my work. I asked if they would be willing to write a letter to their current or former coach. With much enthusiasm, they agreed. The first set of letters were eye-opening. This first request led to a deluge of unsolicited letters from athletes who heard about the development of this book. It was evident: athletes craved to have their stories heard likely because we've silenced them for far too long.

You are about to read a diverse collection of confidential letters from thirty athletes written to their coaches answering one question: *What do you wish you could have told your coach but, for whatever reason, never did?*

Whether you are a youth, high school, club, NCAA Division I, II, or III, NAIA, professional, or Olympic coach, you've opened the right book. But before diving into these letters, I would like you to know a few things. First and foremost, the letters in this book represent an expansive athlete population from various sports,[8] competition levels,[9] and demographic backgrounds. Thus, the claims in this book are not prescriptive; instead, they are overarching, general considerations we need to discuss if we want to make positive changes in sport. Additionally, for confidentiality purposes and athlete safety, I removed all identifying information,[10] altered the storyline of some of the examples provided, and used gender-neutral language.

Moreover, while I ideally wanted to present untouched athlete letters, light copyediting was performed to ensure clarity and consistency, and to make for an easier read. Please note, I preserved the original content and meaning of each athlete's letter. Other than requiring participating athletes to be above the age of eighteen, I set no rules. Thus, I got *real* responses—raw letters filled with emotion.

Second, I set this book up into three simple parts. In Part I, you'll read athlete thank-you letters (the good) to ease you into Part II (the not-so-good). After you read each letter, I offer space for you to empathize and reflect on each athlete's truth. If you're someone who likes to write in the physical copy of the book, I suggest you highlight, circle, or underline important aspects of each letter that stands out to you. Write notes in the margins. If you're unlike me and don't like to write in your books, have a journal handy as you read. Make notes about what you believe you should start doing, stop doing, and keep doing based upon what each athlete shares.

All I ask is that you approach these letters with an open mind and willing heart—not only to do better by athletes but also by yourself. To honor every athlete, sit silently with each letter and let their experience speak to you. Once you've learned what you need to learn from one letter, move to the next.

After reading all the letters offered in Parts I and II, you may expect to find a list of solutions in Part III. Instead, I simply provide a different truth. Hearing athletes' voices is only the first step in a much-needed conversation among all members of the industry: athletes, coaches, academics, and administrators. So, in Part III, I invite you to take the next step in the conversation. I share my own Dear Coach letter and invite you to write your own. After all, coaches are developed by other coaches, and I'm willing to bet every coach has a Dear Coach letter to write.

One final note: This book challenges fundamental tenets on which sport is built. Thus, I ask that you detach from how you've been socialized into sport as you read so you fully can imagine along with us a system where sport is safer for all, both the athlete *and* you. So, while, yes, I wrote this book to give athletes a platform to share their stories, I also wrote this book for you, Coach. I started this journey because coaches wanted to know what athletes thought. You are a vital component in the coach-athlete relationship. Yet, we've done a relatively lousy job of advocating for you as well. I believe you, the coach, deserve more. You deserve to know the good and the not-so-good, from the vantage point of the athlete, so that we can make the world a better place together through sport. Thank you for your willingness to take this journey with us.

PART I:
The Good

LETTER
1

Dear Coach,

I know that I thanked you at the end of my final season with you, but I don't know if I did a really good job of telling you why. You were always so good about giving me positive feedback immediately after practice or a competition, but I failed you in that regard. I often would just say, "Thanks," in a fairly unemotional way and then move on. So, here's a detailed account of why you were the best coach.

First and foremost, thank you, for being the chill-est [person] at the competitions. Of course, I was always fairly high-strung. The fact that you were so chill really gave me a reference point for what I needed my energy to be, so I stuck with you [on game days] because I needed your chill energy to rub off on me. I was always perplexed by how chill you were, though, because I knew you were stressed. You had a lot going on at home, a [family member] who was dealing with cancer. You must have been so sad to miss all that precious time with them because you had to be with us so much. Even with that stress, though, we could never tell. You were always so good about when you were with us, you were just with us. That, to me, is the definition of mental toughness.

I not only want to thank you for being the energy that I needed on game days but also for trusting me. I've [competed] under coaches who were super stressed out on game days, which made me feel that they didn't trust my abilities to compete well. Because you were so calm, I knew it was because you trusted me. That freed me up to perform better than I ever had. I felt mentally stronger than ever before. Reflecting upon our time together, I truly feel that's because you showed us what it was supposed to look like. You exuded mental toughness, so it was easy for us to become it.

Although I did perform well under your coaching, there were those [competitions] that I bombed. I can't tell you how much it meant to me that you still came up to me and said, "While that wasn't your best performance, here are all the things you did well." That caught me off guard because I was so used to the coaches I had before you either yelling at me or ignoring me completely. Not you, though. After you listed off all the things I did well, I remember you saying, "Okay. Now, try this a little more." You gave me big praises and little constructive criticisms, which, now I understand, allowed me to better digest what I needed to do.

Coaches before you always did the opposite. They would (maybe) tell me one or two things I did right and then lay into me about all the things I did wrong. It was overwhelming. I didn't know where to start, which often led to me questioning why I was even competing in [sport] in the first place. But with you, you made my areas for improvement more digestible. You overwhelmed me with praise and gave me one or two things I needed to work on moving forward, often asking me which one I thought was more important so we knew what to work on first. You didn't just leave it at that, though. You sat with me. We came up with a game plan together for how we were going to accomplish these areas of improvement. You coached me, but you also gave me some space to coach myself.

I remember the day that you were coming up with the practice schedule for the next week. You asked us, "What time would you all prefer to show up [at practice]?" I was a little floored because the coaches I had before you would just tell us when practice was, and we would show up. With you, you gave us a say. We sat in your office and had a group discussion about the best time for all of us to have practice. I argued for 7 a.m. because that's when I performed best. Some other athletes argued for 11 a.m. because they wanted more time to sleep in. After a little compromise, we settled on trickle-in scheduling. That is, you said you would open the [practice facilities] at 8 a.m. For those who wanted to come in earlier, we could arrive at 8:00. For those who felt they needed a little more sleep to perform better, they had to arrive to the gym by 10:00.

You then staggered the coaching staff's schedules to ensure a coach was present at all times. Obviously, we had the coaches we preferred to work with; however, you offered the option that if a coach we wanted feedback from wasn't at practice, we could record ourselves practicing and send the video files to that particular coach to analyze. While there were pros and cons to this type of practicing style, I think there were more pros than cons. One con was that if the coach I wanted to observe my practice wasn't present, I wasn't able to get the immediate feedback. However, I really appreciated how you let us have a say in what time worked best for us to practice. I think it protected me from creating some kind of subliminal resentment toward you. It also offered me opportunities with other coaches that I wouldn't have sought out myself. I gained more respect for the coaching staff as a whole. I also gained differing viewpoints on what each coach thought I should work on.

For some, this might have been overwhelming—having too many opinions about what to work on thrown at you—but you were always so good about empowering me to determine what I thought I needed to work on. Whatever I said, that's what you championed.

Sometimes I get asked why I competed so well. I won many championships under you. I've given differing answers across the years, but I've finally settled on one: Coach, I did so well competing under you as a coach because we were both coaching. It was me and you coaching me. You always gave me a say in how I thought I was competing from a technical standpoint, and you also gave me voice in how I thought the game strategy should go. You revised and edited my opinion based on your expert knowledge, but you never wavered in letting me make additions, edits, or revisions. It was very back and forth in that way. You supported me. You wanted to share my vision, so you valued communication with me. I am happy to know that there are people like you out there. It's encouraged me to be the same for others.

Letter 1: Reflection

What stood out to you in this athlete's letter?

_____

_____

_____

_____

_____

_____

_____

What could you incorporate into your coaching as a result of reading this athlete's story?

_____

_____

_____

_____

_____

_____

_____

_____

_____

LETTER
2

Dear Coach,

Even putting the word "coach" in the header is weird to me. Although I am still currently an athlete, I haven't used the word "coach" in a long time. The coaches I've had didn't give that word a good connotation. I've worked with every type of coach you could imagine:

- The dictator,
- The pushover,
- The "buddy" coach,
- The "my way or the highway," and of course,
- The coach that's literally your [parent].

Every single kind of coach handled me differently, probably because I wasn't the easiest to handle. I cuss. I fight. I party. But I showed up every single day ready to perform. Those before you saw the former traits. You saw the latter because you were able to empathize. Every player has their stuff: family issues, trouble at home, [significant others], and kids. Most coaches don't care unless it affects performance. I never brought my issues to a coach before because, when I did, I was always told the same thing: "You need to find a way to separate the game from your life."

I heard that message so much that I learned it was just best to hide everything. I did what every "good" athlete was supposed to do, which was shut out my problems.

When you became my coach, though, I heard stories about you before we even met. I already labeled you the "dictator" type. Jokingly, I asked you when we were going to fight in the octagon. You quickly fired back, not too happy about my comment. It caught me off guard, and I thought to myself, *Well, that's not a good start.* I figured I was in for a long season, but that changed when, a couple weeks into the season, you called a meeting. I figured it was another meeting the team puts on to help us "grow as an [adult]." The mood was different in the room that day, though. You told us your story. You opened up as a person; you confided in us. I had never seen that from a coach before. As you went on with your story, I couldn't help but feel horrible. Not because I felt bad for what had happened to you (which, don't doubt, I do) but because I finally felt like I saw you as [your name] and not just [Coach, your title]. By sharing your story, you gave me perspective—perspective I had not had throughout my entire career in any sport.

After that meeting, you told us that your door was always open. It was the first time I believed it when a coach said that. A few days later, you proved yourself right. I found myself coming into your office a couple times a week [to share my story]—a story not many have ever heard. You taught me how to handle my emotions. You taught me how to be an [adult] and handle my business. You gave me a hug when I needed it and a tough, encouraging nudge when I was feeling sorry for myself. I guess what I'm trying to say is thank you. You kept me in the game way longer than I thought I would be. Without you in my life, I don't know where I'd be—probably miserable in some office because I gave up on my dream. It was an honor to get to play for you. We won championships because of your leadership. That was the closest team I have ever played for, all because of you.

Letter 2: Reflection

What stood out to you in this athlete's letter?

_____

_____

_____

_____

_____

_____

What could you incorporate into your coaching as a result of reading this athlete's story?

_____

_____

_____

_____

_____

_____

_____

_____

LETTER
3

Dear Coach,

It's been over three years since I was first coached by you, and to this day, my best memories of being an athlete for a team came from being under your tutelage. You were more than just a coach to me. You were a mentor, an athletics coach, a life coach, and a huge motivator to not settle for anything less than my best. To this day, I still hold the last words you said to me before what I still consider to be my best competition: "You've trained hard; there's no reason you can't beat these other athletes." Similarly, I also remember the words you said to me four days before that competition, during a workout: "If you compete like that, they're going to drop you!" You knew the perfect balance of being a tough coach but also an empathetic and patient coach.

When I talked to you for the first time at one of my previous competitions, I instantly knew that no one else was as passionate about the sport as you were. The way you analyzed the Xs and Os, I was convinced that you would be the coach to get me to the national level. I was excited to join your ranks, and I could not wait to prove myself to you. I made mistakes during my first season under you, but through that, you supported me and never gave up on me. You also were never afraid to ask the question many coaches are afraid to ask: "Why'd you compete like that?" After giving my response, you would be quick to tell me not to dwell on this competition but rather shift my focus to the next competition.

You were never afraid to correct the way I would think either. When I told you I wanted to compete in a certain way to get the outcome I wanted, you would be quick and unafraid to say, "Forget about that; focus on the process of being competitive with the opposition." You'd say, "If you do that, the outcome will take care of itself." To this day, that's still the thing that goes through my mind when I'm about to compete. You always told me that I was my worst enemy and my worst critic when it came to competing, and because of that, I would psych myself out. You were the one who taught me to be hard on myself and keep myself accountable, but you taught me to do it in a way where I didn't put myself down. You taught me to reflect on a competition, pinpoint what I did wrong, and work on that weakness, but you also taught me that my value wasn't in the numbers. You saw me as more than an athlete. You saw me as a hardworking human being who would be just as disappointed as you if the competition didn't go as planned.

I still remember that one competition we barely lost. I remember thinking about how pissed you were going to be. After the competition ended, you came looking for us. I remember hearing you say to my teammates, "Where are they [referring to me and my teammate]?!" I came up to face you, and all you said to me was, "We're going to work more on what you were lacking today because I know you have it in you." Even though you never really chewed me out after a competition, no matter how bad, I expected this one to be the first. Instead you very calmly told me what we needed to work on. I thank you for that.

Beyond being a sport coach, you were also a life coach in my eyes. I remember riding with you to and from practices where you shared about your experiences as a student-athlete. You shared your family traditions, your family's way of thinking, how they raised you, and why they raised you like that. You were never afraid to open up about your upbringing. You talked about how the sport you coached was big in your family, and how you felt a lot of pride for that. You competed at the institution you now coach at. I remember you telling me how you weren't one of the most talented athletes on the team, but you were the hardest working and most committed athlete there. I take that to heart because that's exactly how I feel. At the end of those talks, you would always tell me what you learned from your experiences, and how you used them to propel you forward. You would then tell me what I could learn from it as well. This made me feel like I could share myself with you, so I started to open up to you about my upbringing. I told you how I was raised and why my parents raised me like that. It really strengthened the relationship I had with you, which made me want to put so much more effort into our sport, not just for myself but for you, too.

But we didn't just talk about our backgrounds; we talked a lot about the sport and about some of the best competitors and coaches in the history of the sport—albeit with some disagreements and even arguments. But even through the arguments, you still made it a safe environment for me to share my opinion. Through the personal anecdotes you shared about your life, you taught me not to take anything for granted, especially those closest to me, and you also taught me the values of hard work and not giving up, even through adversity. This wasn't just for sport but for life as well.

More than that, you changed me from when I first came into your program. When I first came in, I was extremely obsessed with the sport. I obsessed because I believed that being in the sport and being accomplished in the sport was what determined my worth as a human. When I didn't do sport, I hated life. I would be depressed if or when I wasn't able to do my sport. To this day, I still love and need the sport. However, you made me realize that there's more to life than sport. You taught me that during the transition periods, I should have fun. I should eat as much as I wanted, stay up later, go out more, and just generally enjoy my time off. Transition periods are still my least favorite because I still hate not being able to do the sport. With that being said, I can now enjoy myself a little more during those periods. I don't feel guilty if I eat out a little more or stay up a little later or go out significantly more. You taught me what was necessary to be able to come back into training fresh and more motivated.

In one season, you not only changed me as an athlete but also as a person. The numbers I produced were better after only four months of your training. I remember one of my teammates came up to me very frequently during the summer, asking me questions. One day they asked me a question that I could not answer myself. I told them that they should ask you, the coach. Their response was, "I don't want to approach the coach because of [my lack of abilities]." I told my teammate that you didn't care [about their athletic abilities], that you would help them regardless. My teammate built up the courage to talk to you, and I remember them telling me afterwards that I was right, that you truly helped all athletes, [no matter their athletic ability].

I thank you for giving not just me but all my teammates, from the top athlete to the athlete still trying to find a reason to continue in the sport, 100 percent. I don't know how many athletes will say that you changed their perspective on many things for the better, but I know that your tough love was fundamental to growing my mindset and getting me better in the sport. The thing about tough love, though, is that I've heard coaches calling it "tough love" when they were being tough, but they forget to love. You earned the right to be tough because you showed love first and foremost. You were empathetic with not just me but all of the athletes you worked with. In two years, you taught me more than most coaches teach in four or five years of having an athlete. You taught me lessons that I still carry with me to this day—lessons I will carry for life. You further fueled my passion for the sport and my desire to be a coach in the future. The lessons you taught me will also be the lessons I teach the athletes I hope to have the privilege to work with in the future.

Letter 3: Reflection

What stood out to you in this athlete's letter?

_____

_____

_____

_____

_____

_____

_____

What could you incorporate into your coaching as a result of reading this athlete's story?

_____

_____

_____

_____

_____

_____

_____

_____

LETTER
4

Dear Coach,

Thank you. Thank you for everything you ever did for me and those around us. You demanded the best out of every one of your athletes within the sport, classroom, and life. Within the sport itself, you believed we could all be champions—every single one of us, from the kid who joined that year to the kid who was already established as one of the best on the team. You believed we were all better than we ever saw ourselves. In life, you didn't allow us to be entitled. You didn't allow our backgrounds to determine if we played or not. And when we acted out? You humbled us. I remember one kid who decided to put up a number one after winning, which [this player] coupled with an attitude that they were entitled to that gold medal. After that competition, you humbled them in such a way that they learned to never act that way again. From the kid who had nothing to the kid who had everything, you treated everyone on the team like we were family. For those who were on a bad path, you tried to save and change their ways. I remember seeing a kid who ran around with a bad crowd, always in trouble, and grades as bad as they come. You pushed [this athlete]. You changed [them]. After just one year in your program, [they were] already avoiding that crowd, in significantly less trouble, and passing all [their] classes. You raised the standard of what we could achieve and who we could be. You held us accountable by checking on our grades, even with our teachers. If we were struggling, you found us help. If we had a problem, your door was always open.

For those who were on a good path, you tried to teach them more. You tried your best to be a [parent] figure to all of us. When we needed help or needed guidance, you were always there to help. One teammate was in your office near every day. This was someone I was close to and I remember asking [them] one day what you both always talked about. There was some talk about the sport and practices, but there were also questions about life, friends, significant others, or even how to be a better human being. Everything you taught us and everything you demanded from us was always for the bigger picture. You're known for being the loudest individual in the gym, but not many knew how quiet you could be to us. You would yell, scream, and chew us out when we weren't doing our best, but come the end of the day, you always gave us a hug, told us we got better, and told us you were proud of us.

You always demanded more from us because you knew each of your athlete's potential. From the outside it looked like you were just some prick of a coach yelling at your athletes, but here's the important piece that separated you from the rest. We all hear about those coaches, the pricks. They yell and scream, and they leave it at that. You, on the other hand, didn't leave it at that. First, your yelling and screaming was because you were championing us. You believed in us. When I didn't do well, you passionately yelled because you saw better in me, which I began to see in myself as well. But, when the [competition] was over, you approached me to reflect and discuss future game strategy. While other coaches, when an athlete didn't do well, might just ignore the athlete after a match, you still acknowledged us. It was unconditional in that way. We knew, no matter what we did, we would never disappoint you. I believe that is what separates the good from the great coaches—those who unconditionally coach.

I still remember losing a competition and not performing as well as I should have. You gave me an ear full of a lecture, but come the end of the day, you had your arm around me telling me how proud you were of me and how I got better that day. To a few of us, you were a coach. To many of us, you were a [parent] figure. Thank you. Thank you for making me a better athlete by always pushing me and demanding more from me. Thank you for making me a better student by pushing me to have better grades, even when I was passing all my classes. But most important, thank you for making me a better individual, for showing me how to treat those around me. You showed me the importance of putting time into everyone, no matter who they were. When we didn't perform to our potential, you were heartbroken—heartbroken but never disappointed. You viewed us as champions, even though we might not have necessarily thought of ourselves in that way at times. We all saw how much every loss hurt you, which only helped us realize our own potential more. We all wanted to win for ourselves, but we also wanted to win for you. You caused us to believe in ourselves.

In a town rampant with sport politics, you stayed true to coaching. You took a lot of heat and a lot of pressure for it, but at the end of the day, you cared about us as people more than you cared about our last name on the back of our jerseys or how much money we brought the program. You taught me to have integrity and honesty in everything I do by not letting politics rule your coaching. To the best coach I have ever had, *thank you!* You made me want to play for you and win for not only myself but for you as well. You always made me feel like someone cared about me, regardless of outcome. You pushed me to be the best athlete I could be. You pushed me to work harder. You gave me a mindset to approach success, not only in sports but in all aspects of my life as well. The [person] I am today and the [person] I will be in the future is heavily influenced by you. Thank you, Coach, for allowing me to feel like family. To me, you will *always* be a part of my family.

Letter 4: Reflection

What stood out to you in this athlete's letter?

_____

_____

_____

_____

_____

_____

_____

What could you incorporate into your coaching as a result of reading this athlete's story?

_____

_____

_____

_____

_____

_____

_____

_____

LETTER
5

Dear Coach,

Since the age of four, I wanted to go to the Olympics. Every day I would wake up envisioning myself with [my country's flag] on my chest. To me, the Olympics represented more than just a stage of ultimate athletic excellence; it represented opportunity and hope. My sport taught me that hope is not a passive daydream but rather a call for action. If I hoped to go to the Olympics, I had to work to make it happen.

Since the age of seven, I started training thirty hours a week, which required me to attend school part time. My daily regime consisted of school, practice, homework, sleep, repeat. I missed many birthday parties as a child and many high school parties as a teenager. Younger than most, I started ordering a "side salad and water" versus "French fries and a milkshake." My sport taught me that to be good, you had to work hard, but to be excellent, you had to sacrifice.

Since the age of twelve, I claimed the status of being an elite athlete and three years later earned a spot on [my country's] national team. I remember receiving a call saying, "[My country] has just released their list of national team athletes, and I could not be prouder to tell you that your name is on that list." My sport taught me about the concept of community. Growing up in a single-parent household, I learned that my grand[parent] gave my [parent] one hundred dollars every month until the day they passed and would say, "This [child] has a dream, not many people dream like that." I wrote letters to local businesses that ended up funding my training. I had members of our town drive me to and from practice every week in the middle of their day because my [parent] had to work. I may have been the one doing the [sport], but it took a community to get to that point.

One particular year, I was named on the list of [my country's] athletes from which they were going to pick the Olympic Team. Sadly, I was not chosen. This is where you came in, Coach. The following year, I stepped foot on campus, a first-generation college student with a full-ride scholarship to your program. I may have thought my dreams were to attend the Olympics, but you showed me that my dreams could be much bigger than our sport itself.

During my first year, I experienced an unexpected setback that I could have never imagined, one often accompanied by words like "insurmountable," "devastating," and "career ending." I had to relearn every skill in my repertoire and get back to the level of sport that you recruited me for. At the end of our season, you told me I had two months to prove myself before I could sign my scholarship renewal. You said that this was going to be one of the hardest things I would have to do as an athlete, but if I wanted it bad enough, I would make it happen. I walked out of your office and straight into the weight room. From that day on, I completed every request of yours in practice and walked right back into the weight room for an additional workout. Day one, I felt defeated. Day two, I was more tired and sore than I had ever been in my life. Day three, I felt a little stronger.

Six weeks later, I signed my scholarship renewal. When the next season rolled around, I realized I was never going to be the anchor for our team, but you reframed this realization for me by helping me understand that my role was still vital. You tasked me with bringing consistency to the [competition]. You never failed to emphasize that this role was just as important. You helped me become the athlete who stepped into competition feeling invincible and in complete control. You transformed me from being an athlete who feared failure to an athlete who craved success. I finished my career as team captain along with being named a three-time Academic All-American and [organization's] Person of the Year Nominee.

Somewhere along this journey, I remember sitting in your office. You said something so profound that it has stuck with me to this day. Maybe you remember this analogy, or maybe it was a moment of unknown significance to you. But it fueled my collegiate athletic career and fuels my ambitions today and for the rest of my life:

In [sport] and in life, you will be facing a mountain that you have to climb. Other people around you will climb straight up, making it to the top in a matter of hours. You cannot control whether or not you are one of those people. In [sport] these are, perhaps, the people who are naturally talented, the athletes who do not get injured, or the athletes who did [experience what you experienced]. Then there are people like you, who, to get to the top of the mountain, have to take every single winding path, going up and down, around and around. This may take you days, weeks, or months, and it can be challenging and frustrating when you see others pass you. If you just keep moving forward, though, one day you will make it to the top of the mountain, and when you are at the top, you will be grateful for your journey.

Thank you, Coach.

Letter 5: Reflection

What stood out to you in this athlete's letter?

_____

_____

_____

_____

_____

_____

_____

What could you incorporate into your coaching as a result of reading this athlete's story?

_____

_____

_____

_____

_____

_____

_____

_____

_____

LETTER
6

Dear Coach,

Thank you for everything that you did for me during the last three and a half years we were together. We both came in together, you as the new head coach and myself as an athlete, with no idea of what was going to happen. Both of us were learning how to survive that first year. At least you had life experience on me, so it was probably a little easier for you to adjust. For me, it was difficult. I was just keeping my head above water, barely staying up. I got shoved back under water when I found out about my parents' divorce. At first, I did what I thought I was supposed to do. I put up the mask so others couldn't see what was happening on the inside where I was paddling aggressively to stay afloat. You and the psychologist I worked with were the only people who saw me put out any emotion that year. Because you showed that you cared about my life outside of sport, I came into your office like clockwork just to chat. Every Monday we would chat for an hour about anything. Sometimes we talked about what I had going on personally. Other times we would talk sports, about the state of the team. You asked my opinions about how I thought we were doing and really took my thoughts to heart. You asked what we could do moving forward, which allowed me to grow and learn. These meetings empowered me to grow into the adult I am today because you taught me what it means to be a leader.

Much of the reason why I want to get into coaching is because of how you led. While there are some things I fully didn't agree with or like that you did, overall I still think you were great. For instance, my teammates and I complained about how we were always on time to practice, something that you preached, but you were always late. It was the small things that we would get annoyed with because I would have liked for you to hold yourself to the same standard you held us. But, when it came to the major things, you were always there.

One thing I really learned from you, and I hope I can carry on, was being open to your players. You were so approachable. If someone had an issue, they could come to you. Because of your openness, I knew you cared about me. So when we went on the field, I would listen to what you had to say because of the respect I knew you had for me as well as the respect I had for you. If there were ever any disagreements between you and us, we could voice our opinions, but ultimately, we knew you had our best interest in mind when you made the final decision. There were no questions about that.

I can write for days about things that I really respected about you, but the one thing that comes to mind immediately is how you valued family. You would always make a point of doing things for your kids and making sure you were there for their activities, like going to dances with your daughter or to your son's baseball games. I was observing all of it and understanding how I wanted to handle the intersection of business and life.

Here's what really meant the most to me, though: you and I would go out to the field by ourselves and just [play recreationally] for an hour. When I become a coach, I want to do stuff like this with my players. Not only did it help me with the technical side, but we were also able to talk about stuff. We connected in ways we had not by just chatting up in your office. In my opinion, this allowed our relationship to grow. So, never doubt: you were just what I needed at that moment of my life. Most [people] I know hated their coach and had no respect for them. Not all the [athletes] may have liked you, but one thing's for sure: we all respected you.

Letter 6: Reflection

What stood out to you in this athlete's letter?

_____

_____

_____

_____

_____

_____

_____

What could you incorporate into your coaching as a result of reading this athlete's story?

_____

_____

_____

_____

_____

_____

_____

_____

_____

LETTER
7

Dear Coach,

Thank you. I think that is something you don't hear enough, so I wanted to take this opportunity to say it again in more depth. Thank you for everything you have done and still do for the athletes you coach. You spend an unbelievable amount of time every day doing things that many people don't see. Shoot, you even did all of our workouts before we did so that you were always able to say you would never have us do anything you wouldn't do. Little things like that didn't go unnoticed. It showed us your character, which ultimately helped build a great foundation for the team culture you helped create and the relationship I had with you.

I will forever cherish the years of playing on your team, which revolved around the culture you helped create. Past, present, and future athletes feel as if they are family due to that culture. I never questioned how much you truly cared for our team. How did I know you truly cared for us? I think the most obvious way is how you trusted us with your own family. You basically shared them with us. You would bring them to matches and then have us over at your house for team dinners, which ultimately created a culture of openness and trust. It made me feel safe. You trusted us enough to play games with your [kids] and that trust transcended into practices. Since you trusted us, we trusted you. We trusted your plan. Even if we didn't always agree with it, we knew there was a purpose to every drill and every line-up. Training for conference play each year was a journey that had quite a few lows but many more highs. All of those highs were because of the incredible coach that you are. You believed in all of us and with each passing day helped us become stronger in just about every way.

I also want to thank you for knowing practice doesn't always have to be so serious. I believe we perform at our best when we enjoy what we are doing, and, Coach, you helped bring that enjoyment to the court. I'm not going to pretend like every practice was full of fun because there were plenty of days that were frustrating and discouraging, but even on those tough days, we knew you truly wanted what was best for us. There were also all the really fun times at practice, like on Halloween. Getting to wear costumes to practice and play games would reignite the joy we had for the game and strengthen the connections everyone had with each other. It gave us a practice just to have fun. It was incredible; I will forever remember those practices with pure joy.

Now, on to the more serious stuff: September 25, 2014, a day I will never forget. We were scheduled to depart that afternoon for a tournament. The morning of, I found out my grand[parent] had passed away. I honestly didn't know how I was going to make it on the trip or perform that weekend because my mind was not ready to compete. A teammate shared with you that [my grandparent] passed away that morning and how difficult it was for me to handle. Looking back, it was definitely one of the hardest days I have endured in my life. I remember showing up to the vans that day, not knowing how to share the news without breaking down, but you already knew. You came up to me, said all the right things, and gave me a hug. This is what you told me:

1. It was okay to be upset.
2. I had the support of everyone on the team.
3. The weekend was an opportunity for me to go out and play for my grand[parent]; win or lose, [they] would be watching over me as I took the court.

Hearing these words from you reminded me of my [grandparent's] competitive spirit; when my [sibling] and I used to play together, [my grandparent] would always say, "Stomp on them when they're down and don't let them back up!" Followed with, "Go get 'em, Tigers." For the entirety of the tournament, I kept replaying in my mind the saying, "Go get 'em, Tiger." And although I knew I would never hear [my grandparent] say those words again, they would remain with me forever. So, Coach, thank you for allowing me the time to grieve the loss of my grand[parent] and still have the opportunity to go out and compete alongside my teammates. You taught everyone on that day that it is not always about winning or losing but enjoying our time doing the things we love. For those moments, I will be forever grateful.

Last (but definitely not least), thank you for always having faith in me, even when I didn't. Thank you for trusting me, even when I had my doubts. Thank you for helping me become the individual I am today. During my time with you, I was fortunate to figure out what I wanted to do with my life; I knew I wanted to have an impact on people, just as you had an impact on me. You were one of the first people I called when I was hired for a full-time job because playing for you gave me the opportunity to find my passion, which has lead me to where I am today.

I'll finish with this: inspiration comes in many different forms and modalities, and you are that inspiration to me. You were the fuel to our team's fire, so thank you for lighting the fire within each of us. You showed us the importance of connection, love, and trust through your coaching style, which I've brought with me into my professional life. Coach, you have had such a significant impact on my life, and I am eternally grateful for the experiences we had. One day, I will meet someone I will want to spend the rest of my life with. I look forward to the day I see you at my wedding with your family and the rest of our team.

Letter 7: Reflection

What stood out to you in this athlete's letter?

_____

_____

_____

_____

_____

_____

_____

What could you incorporate into your coaching as a result of reading this athlete's story?

_____

_____

_____

_____

_____

_____

_____

_____

_____

LETTER
8

Dear Coach,

I want to thank you for all you have done for me. I wish you could see yourself through my eyes. You would see how wonderful, heroic, dedicated, passionate, and looked up to you are. You are wonderful because you are like a second [parent]. It can be hard for an eighteen-year-old to come into college, leaving their family and not having anyone. You are that for me and for all the other [athletes]. You are a hero when you stay up all night on the bus when the weather isn't the best, just to make sure we make it home safely. You are dedicated and passionate when you give us our scouting reports and watch endless hours of film. You are looked up to for how you can balance everything between a family, twenty [athletes], and a job.

I understand that to coach is a sacrifice. You may not always make the amount of money you want to. You have to give up special moments with your kids. You work hours upon hours watching film to prepare for one game. You give up so many aspects of your life to ensure that we as your athletes feel prepared. You do this all for one game, which is the biggest thing that we have in common: this one game. You and I are working toward one single goal, and that is to win. It doesn't matter our background, our age, our thoughts. This one game has brought us together to work for something bigger.

I also want to thank you for building me into the person that I am. You pushed me to graduate. You checked on me weekly. You went above and beyond to make sure I knew you were there for me. You took the time out of your day to have a meeting with me almost every week to make sure I was on track to graduate, had the tools that were necessary, and was in contact with whomever I needed to be to be successful. I find it amazing that you were able to see when one of us was struggling and somehow make us smile. I remember one [athlete] on our team was struggling with something personal, and after practice, you pulled them aside. You were there for them as support but also as a person simply willing to listen. You made it more than just a game.

You have taught me that while we are in college, it may seem that sport is our life, but there is so much more out there for us. You have shown us that the little things don't need to be stressed, that it is okay to have a bad day. But most important, you have given me an escape—an escape from all of the drama, homework, stress of life, injury, and family. You have given me a safe haven where I can walk in, take a deep breath, and forget about life for the next two hours. My parents went through a divorce when I was younger, which made [sport] an escape for me since I was thirteen. You were the first coach to tell me that right before I walked into the [arena] I should take a deep breath. Once my shoes hit that floor, nothing else in the world mattered for two hours. [Sport] has always been my escape, and you made it so that I could continue to have that in college. You have given me memories I will never forget. Laughs, tears, losses, amazing wins, meals, love, support, and everything in between.

I wish you could see yourself through my eyes, Coach. You have changed a lot of athletes for the better. You made us all want to impress you, work for you, and respect you. It didn't matter how we performed at the end of the day. You wanted each and every one of us to grow into strong [humans]. [Sport] was a positive means to the end. You helped me and other athletes build character, stamina, strength, and so much more. Thank you for making this more than just a game. I hope I can do the same thing for a future athlete comparable to what you have done for me. Thank you.

Letter 8: Reflection

What stood out to you in this athlete's letter?

_____

_____

_____

_____

_____

_____

_____

What could you incorporate into your coaching as a result of reading this athlete's story?

_____

_____

_____

_____

_____

_____

_____

_____

LETTER
9

Dear Coach,

Ever since my parents put me in athletics at age four, I wanted to be a professional player and represent [my country]. It was a dream of mine that I was determined to chase after. Whenever anyone would ask me what I wanted to be when I grew up, I would tell them, "A professional sport player." The response would always include a light-hearted chuckle and the statement, "Ha, yeah, what's the backup plan?"

However, this was not the case with you. When I told you what my dream was, all you said was, "Okay, and what are you going to do to get there? . . . What's the plan?" This shocked me because I was not used to having this kind of support. All through high school, you stood by me through the difficult times of sport and life. You taught me so much that no other coach taught me. I learned how to cope with adversity and control what was in my control, which then helped me learn how to find the motivation within myself to accomplish my goals.

Those weekly talks we had about my goals were more impactful than I could have ever imagined. We practiced visualization (the good and the bad in sport) and being more self-aware (especially when my bad temper would try to get the best of me). Even when I would become overly stressed, we would talk about good coping methods to use to calm myself down and attack the problem head-on. I became more resilient. I was able to use these teachings not only in sport but also in life. Even after I was done playing and I asked you for help because I was going to try out at a professional combine, you came to my aid without any hesitation. All I had to do was text you what I wanted to accomplish, and you were quick to respond. You helped coach me through some of the most physically and mentally demanding training sessions I have ever done. You stood by my side. When I would doubt myself and question my abilities, you helped lift me up. You would remind me who I was and what I was capable of doing. You were able to motivate me with just a simple look.

You showed me what a true coach is supposed to be for their athletes. It's not always the wins and losses that matter the most. It's the fight along the way. I have never had a coach genuinely care about me and all my teammates as much as you did. From the team run gatherings every Sunday to just a simple "How are you?" text, I knew you cared about my success as much as I did and that you believed in me (sometimes more than I believed in myself). I looked up to you and still do. I admired the amount of effort you would put into creating a positive environment and building relationships with all the athletes. The impact you left on all of your athletes and me was empowering. You made me want to work harder than I ever have, which led to some of my best performances. When I had a poor performance, you didn't break me down and make me feel terrible about it by blaming me for my failure. You would always first look at yourself to see what you could have done better as a coach. You would help me take the performance as a learning lesson (not every performance is a win) and then move forward to the next challenge. I now use this method of coaching with my athletes, and I couldn't be happier with the outcomes I have had so far.

Thank you, Coach. Thank you for helping to make me the person I am today and who I will be in the future. For the love of the run.

Letter 9: Reflection

What stood out to you in this athlete's letter?

_____

_____

_____

_____

_____

_____

_____

What could you incorporate into your coaching as a result of reading this athlete's story?

_____

_____

_____

_____

_____

_____

_____

_____

LETTER
10

Dear Coach,

Out of all of my former coaches, I have chosen to write to you. I have been able to say what I wanted to the others, but to you, I haven't. This is because you intimidate me the most, which is weird/difficult for me because with all of my former coaches, I have been very close and have befriended them. But with you, it's much harder because of how successful you are. You coach the most successful [sport] program in the nation. You have a ridiculous amount of national titles and coach on the world [sport] team. You are practically a celebrity, which may be why my mind goes blank and I don't have much to say when we do talk.

Being busy all the time has become part of your life, yet you handle it so well. Thank you for that. You are so great at giving everyone the time and attention they need in the moment. These little moments that you and I have together, Coach, are so very special to me, which is probably why I haven't been able to say all of this in those small timeframes. I have never been one to be intimidated or to think so highly of someone after having known them for so long; it's almost like you are another parent that I want to make truly proud of me. I relish the small moments when I can make you proud and receive a hug from you. Our one-on-one time during meetings or practice is most important to me because I have your full attention, as if nothing else matters in the world. Even if they are just meetings about competition plans or future training, you put away your phone and give me that stare where it feels like you are looking into my soul. This is where I, as an athlete, believe 100 percent in our training and what we are doing because I have the world's best coach (whether people think it or not) giving me their full attention.

Throughout my career with you, you have always believed in me. You have especially cultivated and nurtured the thing that is most important to me: my dream of being the best I can be at [sport] and getting the most out of it. As much as I envy or seek your approval as an athlete or person, I cannot thank you enough for coaching me and believing in me. You have your very own kind and fun way of doing it—like the time you told the team (after I had made the national team my second year) that I couldn't run my way out of a wet paper bag the year before. This was the first time I felt acknowledged by you, and it made me feel like I finally started to belong. I wanted to work harder to keep getting your approval and make you proud. That is a memory I will cherish with you forever. You've also encouraged me to keep on dreaming. My first coach planted the seed of chasing my dreams and seeing how far I can take [sport], which made me start to think. My second coach showed me that doubt will always follow, but through hard work and discipline, you can always find success. My third coach showed me what real hard work is and the little things that go into reaching the next level, as well as reminding me about the priceless nature of having fun with teammates at the same time.

Now, to you, my fourth coach: you have shown me how to believe in myself and never think small. I went from thinking, *I could win districts in high school* to *I could compete well in college* to *I think I can compete for [you, Coach]* to *I can be on a national championship team if I compete for something bigger than myself.* You told me after my eligibility was over that I could potentially qualify for the Olympics, which sparked a new wave of thinking in my mind. My thoughts went from thinking I could make the national team to *I could qualify for the Olympics.* Being this close now to qualifying has me thinking about bigger things years down the road. Because of your belief in me, my next thought is this: *I believe I can make the 2028 Olympic team.* So, thank you, for not only pushing me physically but for also helping me nurture a champion's mindset because, without the latter, optimal performance will only go so far.

Letter 10: Reflection

What stood out to you in this athlete's letter?

_____

_____

_____

_____

_____

_____

_____

What could you incorporate into your coaching as a result of reading this athlete's story?

_____

_____

_____

_____

_____

_____

_____

_____

LETTER
11

Dear Coach,

Here, today, I sit and reminisce about the lifestyle you helped me escape. See, it goes like this: A lot of coaches treat players like pit bulls. As long as you can win the fight (the game), they love you, feed you, and make sure you survive. But the moment that dog is defeated, gets injured, and loses the fight, they are no longer valuable. In some circumstances, the dog may even end up dead. After that, life goes on, and they find a new dog. But that wasn't the case with you. You never ever gave up on me. Even when I wasn't winning the fight, you always gave me light. I was always able to tell you anything, and you always understood and helped me be a better me. Even when I was wrong, you got on me, and I could tell you were mad at me just because you *had* to get on me. Does that make any sense?

When you recruited me from [school], I remember talking to you over the phone. I told you what you wanted to hear because, well, I really wanted to play for you. But then, you called one day and told me about yourself, your childhood, your family. That's when I felt I could trust you. That's when I told you about the way I grew up and about my [grandparent]. I told you about me partying, how many partners I had. I was drinking and smoking weed. Back then, they didn't drug test us at [the organization I was at], but you let me know I couldn't be doing that [while I was on your team]. So, I told myself that once I [was playing under you], then I would leave my past in the past. Unfortunately, I dropped dirty. You found out and were so disappointed in me.

I felt you were embarrassed because of how much you bragged about me. I then told myself I would never disappoint you again. Even when I was trying to hide something, you knew I was up to something or something was going on. That is when I knew I could be honest with you just like how I am with my [grandparent] about everything and anything. Then when you and [the other coach] left [the organization to pursue another job], life really started for me. It was the first time, since I was eleven years old, that I would be living without a coach. So, there I was, with no consistent guidance and no real structure, so I started reverting back to my old ways and letting the "hood" catch up to me. But during those moments, you still popped up with quotes and words of wisdom that gave me courage and hope that made me feel I could do anything. You reminded me that I was born to be a star. You told me things like

"Don't get caught up in the world. Let the world get caught up with you!"

"You have greatness inside of you. Bring that light out!"

"Being average is easy. Don't be average!"

"Hey, just checkin' on ya!"

"How's your [grandparent] doing?"

"Write any new songs lately?"

"Keep pushin'. It's your time."

"I'm proud of you."

"Make today great."

"Don't let the negative pull you down and hold you back."

"Keep reaching for the stars."

You sent me these words of encouragement—along with many other inspirational things you said. Those things made me love you, and when you can get a player to trust you, be honest with you, and love you, then that player will do whatever it takes to make you proud [in and out of sport]. That type of relationship brings discipline, commitment, and dedication and makes the player extremely coachable.

Thank you so much for being a coach, friend, [parent], and counselor. Thanks for believing in me during the times it was hard for me to believe in myself and for never giving up on me, even when I wanted to give up on myself. Now, here I am today. The reality is, I'm still on my journey; I'm still reaching for the stars. During this journey, I have gained lots of wisdom and been put in many situations that have prepared me for the next level. Because of you, I will be able to manage the blessing when I'm put in the position to reach the next level.

Thank you, Coach.

Letter 11: Reflection

What stood out to you in this athlete's letter?

_____

_____

_____

_____

_____

_____

_____

What could you incorporate into your coaching as a result of reading this athlete's story?

_____

_____

_____

_____

_____

_____

_____

_____

PART II:
The Not-So-Good

LETTER 12

Dear Coach,

I don't want this letter to come off as hateful because I honestly just want to see change. My goal is to describe the reasons why this letter is written from a critical, not appreciative, lens so as to influence you and other coaches to change the way athletes are treated and to inspire current players to speak up against injustices within their own team cultures.

From the first day you walked in as our new head coach, you promised the world. As a young, impressionable kid, I bought in entirely. You laid out our new mission, used phrases like "commitment to the service of others" or "leaders in our community" and "outstanding citizens." I absolutely loved the direction you were taking the program, and we worked tirelessly toward that mission together, at least at first.

I am not sure when, where, or why the shift happened, but at some point, the mission changed. Not on paper, not in the presentation you gave at the beginning of training camp every year, and certainly not in the words you spoke to the parents of incoming recruits; rather, the change came in how you led our team behind closed doors. To the public, you presented one image. In private, your words did not match your actions.

Suddenly, it was as if the previous mission no longer held value and the only focus was *winning at any cost*. I watched as teammates and I played through injuries—some serious enough to warrant an indefinite sidelining. As teammates, we fought with each other nearly every day, sacrificed opportunities outside of our sport, and dedicated less and less of ourselves to the very reason we were at college in the first place: to get a quality education. We did all of this based on your instruction and in the name of *winning* games. Why? Because that is what we were supposed to do as "good athletes." We were supposed to follow your lead, without question.

As people, our value began to be determined by our ability to help the team *win*. As players, we were only given the time of day when we found a way to be successful and contribute to the culture of *winning*. We were athletes to you, not individuals. You only saw us as machines, and that is the way we began to view each other. The sport we once loved was nothing more than factory work to us now. I started to find my value in my ability to *win*, so if we lost or I didn't play well (which is completely normal), I felt worthless, valueless. Even when we won, it was not enough. The dangerous thing about basing an individual's value solely off winning or losing is the long-lasting effects that linger way beyond sport. I constantly have to remind myself that this experience, which was supposed to be one of the best of my life, was valuable for more than just the connections I made with close teammates. You recruited us by saying that you were going to build people who had a "commitment to the service of others," "are leaders in the community," and "outstanding citizens." But I left your program feeling none of that.

When it was all over, our team won more games in that season than we had in several years. We were one point away from winning the conference championship, the first for our school in over twenty years. Looking at the season objectively, it is clear that we had some success, which might make you, and others looking in from the outside, believe that this *win-at-all-costs* mentality is effective. But because the focus was solely on our ability to *win* more than any other team, many of us look back on the season and feel nothing but disappointment. Even today, I struggle to realize my worth is not dependent upon whether I win or lose, whether I get the grade or land the job. Even right now, I can't help but feel as though I *have* to write the perfect letter because anything less would be an embarrassment to my worth as a human being. Looking back, I wonder how much of an influence you had on my development of this mindset.

If you are a coach reading this letter, understand that we are not pawns to be thrown around at will. Understand that our value goes beyond our ability to *win* [sport] games, that it's an act of negligence to discard, ignore, and move on from us if we are not the best. I hope we can realize that the *win-at-all-costs* approach may result in *winning* on the field in the short term, but it eventually leads to lost confidence, unhealthy mindsets, and distractions from the real purpose of sports, which is a much bigger loss than the numbers on the scoreboard will never be able to capture.

My biggest regret of this entire experience is that I didn't stand up to what was going on. I chose to be a "good athlete" and do what you said, without question. What I didn't understand then, but can see clearly now, is that the "good athlete" you pushed me to be was really just a quiet athlete, one who would produce the best performance with the least amount of resistance.

As I look back on my time with you, I can't help but wish that things had been different. I wish that my value in your eyes was based on more than my contribution to the win. I would have loved to see you value the things that were important to me outside of the game. You talked about family, encouraged community service, and addressed academics. But that is not enough. I needed you to meet the people in my life who were most important to me. I wish you would have been beside us as we jumped in the freezing lake to raise money for charity. Our team needed more than the obligatory grade check once per semester. But, those things didn't directly contribute to winning in your mind, so we didn't get them. The funny thing is, if you had even made an effort to back up the image you presented, then this letter would be entirely different. And I don't think these are impossibly high standards to uphold— maybe just standards that you were unaware existed, although I wish you had cared to ask us what we thought and then maybe you would have known.

Most important, though, I desperately needed open lines of communication. It's not that I think you were deliberately trying to hurt us. Rather, I think you were unaware of the negative impact your actions were having on me and my teammates. I wish you had created opportunities for us to speak up. I needed you to create space where we felt safe to speak our mind for the betterment of the team, instead of just expecting us to blindly commit to whatever direction you decided to throw us in a particular week.

If you are a player who can relate to this type of atmosphere, I want you to recognize that you do not deserve this. You are more than a pawn to be thrown around at will by your coach. So, I wrote this letter, and I stand in solidarity with you, asking that we take our lives back, that we work together to change the culture of sport. As influential as coaches are, the team is ultimately run by the players. *Winning* is neither everything nor the only thing. It is simply a piece of the greater overall meaning of sports: to develop young individuals "committed to the service of others" who are "outstanding citizens" and "leaders in their community." Fight for the values that you believe in. Advocate for yourselves. Let your voices be heard.

Letter 12: Reflection

What stood out to you in this athlete's letter?

_____

_____

_____

_____

_____

If you were the athlete in this situation, how would you react to the coach if you had experienced all these things? What would you do to express your concerns?

_____

_____

_____

_____

If you were the coach in this situation, how would you respond to the athlete if this letter were written to you? Consider your initial reaction as well as any behavioral changes you might make.

_____

_____

_____

_____

LETTER
13

Dear Coach,

I was scared. There seemed to be so much pressure for me to perform—to be the best—that I was relieved when someone outperformed me. I think that's what led me to start each [competition] so hard, which caused me to pass out before it was over. The pressure wasn't necessarily from you, but your encouragement and coaching on top of the internal pressure I felt, well, it just felt like more pressure. You didn't tell me I had to be the best, but the way I saw success was that you are either first or last [thanks to Talladega Nights: The Ballad of Ricky Bobby], and, to be honest, both positions were kind of terrifying. I was scared of success and feared failure, so, ironically, I made both happen in how I competed. I didn't need more (or less) training volume. My tendency to compete to a point of passing out wasn't from lack of physical fitness but lack of mental endurance and fortitude.

Some might think I'm not cut out for sport, given everything I just stated, but really, all I needed was some help in how to get out of my own head. It would have been so helpful to have talked with you about my mental space around [sport], in addition to having the insights and strategies you provided to the physical training. I put a lot of pressure on myself to succeed, and though your encouragement and advice were valuable, they barely stood a chance against my own negative thoughts, self-talk, and perceptions of what was happening. With all of those personal pressures churning around in my head, it was difficult for me to separate my perceptions from your advice, so your advice also felt like pressure.

I eventually went on to play [sport at the next level] with you, and I also struggled with these elements of competition in that setting. I filled in at many different positions and took on various roles on the team. I lifted well. I broke and set weight-lifting records. I trained well. I enjoyed nutrition, exercise, recovery, and skill development. I practiced well, most of the time, but competition, to put it plainly, unnerved me. Again, I know. It sounds like I'm not cut out for sport, but I can't help but think how many other athletes feel the same as me. My lack of self-esteem regarding play and my self-perceptions around competition—in my opinion and in retrospect—kept me from competing well. It wasn't until finding hobbies outside of organized sport, which challenged me and required me to address my lack of self-esteem, that I began to both enjoy and thrive in competition. I believe that engaging in sport helped to lay some foundation for the positive, optimistic mindset I have now. I don't doubt that enduring the physical demands of athletics helped develop the "grit" I'm able to apply to my current endeavors and passions. I so appreciate the lessons I learned through failing and, when in team dynamics, succeeding. Being able to apply those skills to my life feels priceless. I used to be an athlete, but now I'm a competitor, and there's a big difference. I sometimes wonder: how much more could I have enjoyed it and how much better could I have performed had I had some insight to my mental game as much as there were drills for my physical training?

That's what I needed from you. While you were a great coach, I still needed more. I respected your dedication to practices, the thought and consideration that you very obviously put into our training, and your own love of the sport. It was evident in other athletes' success, our [sport] team's success, and even my own physical capabilities that you were well versed in the requirements of a strong physical training program. I needed you to understand that the mental side of competition was getting the better of me, and I could have used support there. I wish there would have been discussion about my emotional and mental states related to competing. I wish I had felt comfortable addressing these struggles with you. That you would have asked what I thought was causing my struggles; where my head was in the middle of all of it. I feel like, had we had those discussions or had the resources been available in that regard, my [sport] "career" would have played out very differently. If we could have game-planned and strategized regarding my head space during/around competition as much as we did the physical elements, I feel like those competitions might have ended more preferably.

I'm grateful for the [sport] advice and insight you offered then. It feels applicable now, and I often hear your advice when I'm training nowadays. It does wonders, seriously. I just wish I had had better cognitive processes around [sport], so that I could have gotten more out of it back then. So, while I say thank you in some regards, I finally want to speak up and say that I needed an advocate. I knew you believed in my skills. I never doubted your dedication to my training. There was no question that you wanted the best for me as an athlete and even as a person at times, but I still needed more. Who we are in our head is who we will manifest, so even if you put all the work into the physical aspect, it will only go so far if our headspace isn't up to par. I needed you to be the first line of defense to see that.

Letter 13: Reflection

What stood out to you in this athlete's letter?

_____

_____

_____

_____

If you were the athlete in this situation, how would you react to the coach if you had experienced all these things? What would you do to express your concerns?

_____

_____

_____

_____

If you were the coach in this situation, how would you respond to the athlete if this letter were written to you? Consider your initial reaction as well as any behavioral changes you might make.

_____

_____

_____

_____

LETTER
14

Dear Coach,

It has been a few years since I called you that, "Coach," and you will always be just that. During my last few days playing in your program and the weeks immediately following, I wanted to sit down and tell you a few things, but for one reason or another, I decided against it. Now, I wish to share with you some of the things that I wanted to say then. I want to make it clear: I am not writing this letter from a place of hate, and I am not dwelling on the past, wishing it was different. However, I believe the things I have to say to you are things you need to hear because your future players may not have the fortitude I had or the social support system I was blessed with. They may need you.

Coach (noun): an athletic instructor or trainer. Though a simple definition, it is not wrong, but you and I both know that a coach is so much more. A coach is not just a coach. A coach is a mentor, a role model, a parent figure. A coach is a leader, someone to turn to during uncertain times who helps bring certainty to the situation. Being a coach does not end when the practice is over. A coach is each of these descriptions whenever we, the players, see you. I needed you as a coach, as a mentor, as a role model, and as a parent figure outside of the lines. I reached out to you countless times and countless times you turned your back. I fought my battles with every ounce of strength I had, and you forced me to fight against you as well.

You see, a player is not just a player. A player's usefulness does not begin and end with the number of wins they can contribute. A player is a person. Now, let me be clear. I am not saying that you should have been involved in every aspect of my life or coddled me. You need to be tough as a coach, and we need to be tough as players. If we are not tough enough, we better adapt. I get it, but there is a fine line. We need to struggle. We need to face adversity, and, at times, we need to face that adversity alone to learn self-reliance and to develop resilience. But, there also comes a time when the challenges are too big to battle alone. In those times, we need other people to share in the struggle, share in the adversity, and unite as a team. It is called synergy, which happens when the combined effect is greater than the sum of separate effects. In some battles, the effects of synergy are the only way to win the fight.

I was in the hospital, Coach. You knew that. I was not winning the fight. Even though I was in the best hands in the world, I was dying. What kept me going, what kept me fighting was the vision of getting back to the sport I love. What were you doing during that time? You were nowhere to be found—until you called to notify me that you needed my roster spot.

I know our relationship wasn't great, but nonetheless, you were my coach. I looked up to you, and during that period of my life, you were the parent figure. You showed me that, in your eyes during that time, I was nothing more than a chess piece, with the goal being to win games. That just should not happen. I am strong, and despite you, I persevered. I beat my illness, and I made my vision become a reality. But like I said earlier, not all of your players will have the fortitude or social support I had. They may truly need you, and if I am being honest, even with all the other support I had, I needed you.

You need to know it is your responsibility to be there for them. It is like an unwritten contract that we as players listen when you speak. We do as you say. We give everything we have to make your vision come true, but when we face adversity that is bigger than us, you need to help us through it. I am sure that you have seen the effects of this contract failing. You have seen a player who is not pushing themselves as hard as you know they can, a player who starts to not listen to you when you speak or do as you say. What you don't realize is, this player knows that you have broken the social contract. They know that you don't actually care about them as a person. They realize that you will not come to their aid when they face a challenge too great. Because of that, you are not a leader worth following.

So, what am I asking of you? I am asking that you uphold your end of this social contract, that you take a step back and realize that a coach is far more than just a coach. That players are more than pawns in a chess match, and we, the players, as people will give so much more if you can be a leader and mentor for us in between and, often more important, outside the lines. I write this letter for the sake of achieving your vision and for the sake of the next player who needs you.

Letter 14: Reflection

What stood out to you in this athlete's letter?

_____

_____

_____

_____

_____

If you were the athlete in this situation, how would you react to the coach if you had experienced all these things? What would you do to express your concerns?

_____

_____

_____

_____

If you were the coach in this situation, how would you respond to the athlete if this letter were written to you? Consider your initial reaction as well as any behavioral changes you might make.

_____

_____

_____

_____

_____

LETTER
15

Dear Coach,

When you asked me to move across the country to be a member of your team, it was one of the best days of my life. My decision to commit was based on a lot of factors, but the biggest one was the way you made me feel as you recruited me. Things were great, and I really enjoyed my experience up until my world came crashing down [that one night], which happened to be two weeks before my first season on the team. I tore [a major leg muscle] that night, and your first comment to me was that I would be fine and that I should stop being "soft." In reality, I knew before anyone else—just by a gut feeling—that my season had ended. For a second I thought to myself, maybe I am being soft. Maybe I should just walk it off and rub some dirt on it. Fast forward to three days later when I got the results back and was told in your office that I had a surgery and twelve-month recovery ahead of me. I did not think about it then, but I wondered later on, how you must have felt after you heard the results. I never asked, but I would hope the feeling that came up for you was guilt and shame. An apology would have been nice, but all these years later, I forgive you.

The next twelve months of recovery were awful for me. I sat and watched every single lift, practice, and game as my teammates enjoyed every second of being able to participate. Heck, I spent so much time [on the sidelines], I should have been promoted to coach at some point. The worst part about the time I spent [on the sidelines] was the fact that my presence was rarely ever acknowledged. I bet if I did not come to practice or get up for a morning lift, you would not have even noticed. Every once in a while you would pass by me and casually ask, "How are you doing?" My response would always be something like, "Fine, just living the life over here." Your question was always just that though—a box to check off to make yourself feel good. You never once actually sat down with me to ask me how I was *really* doing. If you would have sat down with me just once and genuinely wanted to know how I was doing, here is what I would have told you:

Coach, I am really struggling. This is by far the most adversity I have ever faced in my life, and I am thousands of miles away from my family. I am surrounded by everything [sport], and I can't even participate. I came here to play [sport], and now that has been taken away from me. I cry myself to sleep every night and fight back tears at practices, lifts, and games because I miss the feeling of [getting to play]. I am expected to be at lifts, practices, and games, but half the time, no one acknowledges my presence, which leaves me feeling like a burden. A huge part of my identity was taken away from me. I spend most of my days trying to figure out how to put it all back together, but I can't because it's not my timeline. The doctors have told me I will eventually recover from this, but I will never return as the same athlete again. Now I am worried about how my playing time will be affected even when I do recover. Will I still be able to compete at this level? I am depressed and am starting to isolate myself from the team because all they want to talk about is [sport]. Do you know how hard that is? I avoid calling my family because I have nothing to tell them other than, "Sat on the bench and watched again today; no new news to report here." Do you know how much that breaks my heart? I just want someone to lean on. I want reassurance that everything will be okay because, right now, I feel like the biggest piece of my life is gone, and I have no idea what to do about it.

If you would have taken a second to really check in on me, you would have seen the pain I was going through and maybe someone would have pointed me in the direction of the counseling center eight months earlier than they did. When I returned and played in my first game after ten months of fighting my way back, maybe you would have showed a little bit more excitement than you did. When I had moments where I repeated the same movement that caused my injury and I needed to take a moment, you could have come over to check on me because those moments were terrifying for me. If you had *really* asked how I was doing, maybe my experience would have been different. Maybe I should have told you how I was really doing, but I didn't feel like you gave me the platform or opportunity to do so.

What I will say is this: if another player gets injured and they end up missing playing time, check in on them. But don't just ask how they are doing; *really* ask how they are doing. Show some empathy and make sure their mental health is not suffering from their physical injuries. Give them a job to do to keep their mind busy. Do anything to make them feel like they are still an active member on the team. Make them feel like they have a platform to tell you how they are really feeling. Create relationships with the counseling center and get to know the staff well enough that the referral process is easy. Your athletes may not know they need support in the moment, but they most likely will, so it's in your best interest to be proactive. Have the discussion with the team about mental health and how important it is so we can normalize it. Make sure they know they have a safe space with you to address personal concerns and be prepared on how you will deal with those concerns as they come. My experience with you was not all bad—there were some parts that were good—and I am appreciative of you allowing me to stay on the team throughout my injuries. However, you failed when I needed you the most, so please do what you can so that you do not fail another struggling player.

Letter 15: Reflection

What stood out to you in this athlete's letter?

_____

_____

_____

_____

_____

If you were the athlete in this situation, how would you react to the coach if you had experienced all these things? What would you do to express your concerns?

_____

_____

_____

_____

If you were the coach in this situation, how would you respond to the athlete if this letter were written to you? Consider your initial reaction as well as any behavioral changes you might make.

_____

_____

_____

_____

LETTER 16

Dear Coach,

In an ideal world, I'd like to be able to call or text you when I need advice. I'd like to feel like I can tell you when something big happens in my life. I'd like for your name to be the first one that pops up in my mind when I need a recommendation letter or reference for a potential job. I wish I could invite you to my wedding one day. More than anything, I'd love to be able to consider you a second parent. However, your chilling inability to be authentic, transparent, and personally vulnerable never allowed for us to grow close. On many occasions, you reflected the sentiment that you only saw us as numbers on a roster.

Your failure to see us as human beings in addition to being athletes was appalling. For instance, when a player was injured, instead of incorporating them somehow in practice or welcoming their assistance/feedback as a temporary player-coach, you forbade them from even attending practice sessions, stating that their mere presence resulted in a "distraction" to the rest of the team. You wouldn't even text them back when they had injury updates or questions. Do you know how dangerous this is? You acted as if they were entirely worthless, leading them to believe that their worth is contingent on their ability to perform. Due to your actions, injuries on our team became synonymous with being an outsider—someone who didn't belong. This created the habit of hiding injuries, which would result in greater physical and mental pain down the road.

By the way, we were students too. There is no professional league for our sport after college, so by default, we had to care about our studies. I distinctly remember the practice where a teammate was stressing over an upcoming test and you pulled the athlete aside aggressively in front of the team and yelled at them to leave all distractions outside of practice. I wouldn't necessarily say that, as a student-athlete, our studies should be considered a "distraction" from our sport.

Coach, we were always watching and learning from you. You taught us not to come to you with personal concerns and worries. You taught us that you didn't care to learn who we were. You taught us to bottle things up, probably because that's how you were with yourself. But you should probably know that a person can only keep things bottled up for so long before immense pressure causes them to crack. In the rare instances when we would come to you, you would use condescending tactics and essentially blame our problems on us. When things went awry, we needed you to separate the person from the mistake and be there for us.

You were so concerned with preventing distractions on the team that you never attempted to know who we were outside of practice/competition. Honestly, it made no sense because I guarantee you could've gotten more out of me as an athlete had you known what makes me tick, my likes and dislikes, and my dreams and nonathletic goals. You should have celebrated and cherished the kids you had when you had them. Your job is to coach, yes, but coaching shouldn't stop after putting together workouts and training plans. What I, as a dedicated young person in sport, needed from you was not what I got. I needed fierce authenticity, loyalty, trust, appreciation, vulnerability, and acceptance.

By the time you gave my authenticity a chance and began to trust me, it was too late; I was graduating in two months. I will forever hate that the closest we got came to fruition because of a teammate's hospitalization and subsequent dismissal from the team. Had that teammate's hospitalization not happened, I doubt I would have seen you as a protector with my best interests at heart. If not for that, I'm not sure if I would have ever been able to respect you. How horrible is it that it took a teammate's hospitalization for us to get to that point?

To conclude, to this day, you have never actually acknowledged my sexuality, which is something I really struggled with as a first-year student and grew to accept throughout my time as an athlete. My teammates loved and supported me during this time and [helped me] establish the foundation of my confidence as a gay athlete. You were there to witness my growth yet never spoke of it. Don't ask, don't tell is dead, Coach!

I needed your support, your help, and your care. Why is it that when the assistant coach found out about my sexuality and became an excellent support system and mentor to me, you forbade them from interacting with me? Why did you make me feel so isolated from you and everyone else? I know that you knew about me. Everyone did. It was publicly stated several times via social media, print, and public interactions, yet you never mentioned anything. Being gay doesn't define me, but the act of coming out in an extremely conservative environment was courageous and allowed me to release my anxiety and fears so I could focus on becoming a better athlete. I needed you to acknowledge that, to find a way to celebrate and cherish me as a courageous human. That's when you would have gotten more out of me as an athlete. I hope you are achieving what you truly wanted in life, Coach, because, if you're not, I'm not sure what you're doing in this profession.

Letter 16: Reflection

What stood out to you in this athlete's letter?

_____

_____

_____

_____

_____

If you were the athlete in this situation, how would you react to the coach if you had experienced all these things? What would you do to express your concerns?

_____

_____

_____

_____

If you were the coach in this situation, how would you respond to the athlete if this letter were written to you? Consider your initial reaction as well as any behavioral changes you might make.

_____

_____

_____

_____

LETTER
17

Dear Coach,

I remember coming into my collegiate experience on a personal level with you. I felt close to you. We had things in common. We both had similar backgrounds, a similar sense of humor. We just clicked. But once I started playing for you, that started to shift, and the dynamic of our relationship changed. You became more business oriented. Don't get me wrong; I get it. You needed to facilitate the ins-and-outs of being a coach, which meant less one-on-one time with me. What I didn't expect was, when I arrived, everything you told me would happen isn't how it panned out. You said you wanted me on the team to be a particular kind of player, that I would fill these particular roles in various ways, but when I arrived, you put me in a completely different position. You and I both still know I wasn't naturally a good fit for it, but you put me there anyway. That's when the disconnect and confusion started. As time went on, I remember you asking me if I was okay, and I would naturally just say yes because that's what I felt I was supposed to say. Even though you were verbally checking in on me, which to some might demonstrate your support, your actions up to that point spoke louder.

What you should have asked is this: "How are you fitting into this role? Is there anything you are confused about? What do you think I expect of you?"

I remember sensing that my lack of response [by just saying yes] upset you because you stopped checking in on me. The following year, you expressed disappointment, without saying it, that my effort wasn't where you expected it to be. That offended me and continued to offend me. It became a pattern of disconnect between us. I tried to fill my role as you wanted, but you didn't clearly communicate what that role was, which created more separation between us. I could have really used more communication. Well, I guess I should say *better* communication. I didn't need you just to ask if I was okay, which only gave me the option to say yes or no. I often wonder how you would have responded if I said no in those moments instead of yes. I think there was a 5 percent chance you would have stopped to hear me out but a 95 percent chance you would have been absolutely shocked I responded counter to what you expected me to say. I couldn't take that risk, so I always just said yes, which created more distance. As the distance between us increased, I decided not to tell you about my best friend from back home dying, which significantly impacted my life and performance. You kept asking if I was doing alright, but I had learned that it was safer just to say yeah because it was clear to see that you didn't have the time. You were clearly stressed out yourself.

After a while, I processed enough of my friend's death that I wasn't physically showing much distress on the outside. What you saw wasn't so much stress because of my friend's death but the stress of unresolved resentment toward your lack of concern for me. I know. I know. I didn't tell you about [everything that happened to me]. You had no idea that my life changed, so how was it fair to you? In my head, I knew I needed to tell you so you would know to ask, but because of that preexisting disconnect, in my mind, I questioned why you needed to know. What was going to happen if you knew? Would you have thought I was just trying to give you an excuse for my declining performance? Were you then going to check on me in a way I would have actually liked or been fulfilled by? In my head, I thought probably not because that is not what you showed concern about. You only showed concern for my lack of effort in a position that felt like a lie to me. I know I was disappointing you because you kept saying that I wasn't giving much effort. What you didn't understand is that I was giving 100 percent of what I had in the role I thought you wanted me to fill, and I realized that wasn't what you had wanted in the first place. It just created this air between us, which created even more confusion. I'm exhausted just thinking about it again.

After a year of trying to please you, I realized you didn't get me at all and you didn't even care to try. That was when I realized I didn't want to reconcile the relationship because it would have taken too much energy. To put energy into reconciling our relationship just didn't feel worth it when I was putting so much energy into dealing with the loss of my friend, among many other things. As the years went on, I needed to use my energy to cope with my injury, cope with the loss of my athletic career, and cope with transition into a life where I am no longer an athlete but a professional. All of that took up enough energy for me.

I hated that it came to that, but I had to [get to that point] because you consistently ignored the elephant in the room, which essentially was that we were not connecting but yet we weren't willing to mend to where we could connect. We were just going to say pleasantries, focus on the technicalities we needed to focus on, and that was it. Even though you still made sure that all my ducks were in a row, we were still just communicating in passing.

You quit asking questions that sparked discussions when those kinds of questions were what I thought I was going to get because you had made that attempt when you were recruiting me. That was the difference. I knew you were capable of that level of closeness because you asked those questions in the beginning, during the recruiting process. Once I arrived, though, you stopped asking those personal questions. It was just, "Are you okay?" Which, I get it, you were managing a team at that point. When you were recruiting me, you made me feel so special to the point that I believed I was going to contribute to this athletic program in a way that nobody else could.

It makes sense. It's a great recruiting strategy. That is why recruiting is so important and so much effort is put into it. Other coaches are competing with you, and you are trying to stand out. You initially stood out to me because you connected with me and made me feel like I would be supported when I arrived. While I was supported, it was in a different way. You stopped sharing. It was almost as if you became less of a human and more of just a coach, your label, as I progressed through the years. The more disconnected we became, the more the recruiting process felt like false advertising.

Here's the thing. Even as I say all of this, I understand that you can't be everything for everyone. In my opinion, you shouldn't be because that is just too much for one person to bear. I guess I can't be asking for you to look out for my best interest if I am not looking out for yours, which is why I am writing this letter. You were probably just trying to keep your head above water. You were trying to facilitate a successful team but, unfortunately, not really fulfilling that. You were stressed out. I just didn't want to add another stressor to your plate, which is why I just kept saying *yeah* when you asked if I was okay.

At best, what I needed from you was continued effort. This is what I learned: who we are when we first meet someone isn't who we are after five years together. We have to keep getting to know a person. We have to live with them through the ebb and flow of life. Yes, I wanted you to know my story. I wanted to tell you about my friend's death and everything in between, but I realized it was a two-way street. I didn't feel I could continue sharing my life because you stopped sharing yours. What I wanted was to keep learning about you. It's not just about my story. It's about your story, too. I loved hearing your story during the recruiting process, like how much you loved your dog. Whatever happened to it? What I wanted was to keep learning about your life as it unfolded. Don't just stop with the recruiting process because the longer we went without having those personal interactions, the more it felt like we were strangers. As time passed, I lost sense of who I was playing for, which is what took a lot of the passion out of the performance. I wanted to fight for my teammates and my coach, but that's hard to do when you lose touch.

Letter 17: Reflection

What stood out to you in this athlete's letter?

_____

_____

_____

_____

_____

If you were the athlete in this situation, how would you react to the coach if you had experienced all these things? What would you do to express your concerns?

_____

_____

_____

_____

If you were the coach in this situation, how would you respond to the athlete if this letter were written to you? Consider your initial reaction as well as any behavioral changes you might make.

_____

_____

_____

_____

_____

LETTER
18

Dear Coach,

To be honest, I am still so bitter about how it all went down. At the time, I remember it being so bad that I wanted to reach out to [administration] to tell them the truth about you. I didn't because I remember having a friend who said, "Don't do anything stupid. Don't do anything that can jeopardize or hurt you. Make sure you have the least to lose before you say anything. Wait until somebody asks you to speak, and when it is your turn to speak, then speak up. Don't just go and start shouting because if it isn't your turn to speak and you speak, not a lot of people are going to listen."

At the time, I couldn't disagree, but I was frustrated. I shouldn't have had to weigh the pros and cons. I'm glad I have this opportunity now to write this letter, but I can't help but think, *What if? What if I was never asked to speak?* Then all of that frustration might still be inside of me. I was scared to speak up because I thought I might lose something. It felt like you inherently knew this. It felt like you were always just manipulating the system. Here's what I wish I could have told you then.

Do you remember when you brought in that guest speaker and preached about how this person was like a god? You talked up their story and told us how great they were. They came in and told their story about how they came from a really, really poor family. They had a rough upbringing. They ended up making it, played [sport] in college, and ended up doing really well. I remember listening to the athlete's story and initially thinking, *I can relate, but none of the stuff they did ever measured up to a quarter of what I went through.* After they spoke, I walked up to you afterwards and asked if I could share my story. I wanted to speak in front of my teammates. I wanted to motivate them. You brought this person in and administration paid them money to motivate our team, but you didn't realize you had me on the team. I vividly remember you telling me in your stern voice, "No. I know your story!" And then you quickly dismissed me. Here's the thing: you have never heard my story to know my story. At least you never heard it from me.

Here's what I think you should know. Don't look too far forward for inspiration or too far outside for motivation. As a team, I think of us as one big body that is going to work. You know how you have to be intrinsically motivated to get up every day to go and train? Why not find that motivation within your team? Why not find things in each player on your team to inspire motivation that might help each player find their own self-motivation? I think this motivation and inspiration can be found in the different stories we all have to share. It would have provided us with a broader set of ideas to click with beyond what we were born and raised with, but you made it clear that you didn't care about that.

I know we weren't on the same page politically. I know we weren't on the same page religiously. I know we were not on the same page race wise. We were literally on a different page with every single thing in our life, which you constantly reminded me of. Like that one time you brought up that [religious sport campaign] on television, talking about how inclusive they were being. When you asked me about it [because I identified with that religion], I told you my honest thoughts. I told you I felt like they weren't actually trying to be inclusive. They were trying to *look* inclusive. They were trying to look good on the screen because that's what everyone is trying to do, just look good on the screen. I could tell you were perplexed because you thought I was gonna go along with your views on it.

I could tell you weren't pleased with my stance on the matter when I went on to talk about how it was all just about the money. [This company] saw a great opportunity. They saw that it was becoming trendy to be "diverse and inclusive," so they wanted to come off as the hero to the public. They wanted to send the message that [the company] was inclusive, but they also were making a pretty penny off the oppression of my people. I ended by asking, "What change were they actually making?" That's when you told me that I always blow things out of proportion and should start viewing stuff in a positive light. Let's be honest. You never cared to hear my side of the story because it didn't align with your side, so you just threw it out with the bath water. News flash, your opinion isn't the all-consuming, all-knowing, all-powerful only opinion. If you can't come to understand that, don't ask for my opinion just so you can blow it off because it doesn't align with yours. Honestly, that's a sign of immense immaturity, which is ironic to think about because you always said you wanted to "create us into mature, thriving, optimally performing [humans]." You should look in the mirror because you can't create those humans if you aren't first an upstanding model of those behaviors.

After I spent years with you, it was clear we only had one thing in common: the love for our sport. Even though our differences heavily outweighed our similarities, when we came to play or to practice, why couldn't we all come as a unit? Why couldn't we come with a common goal? We were all building one building, and we wanted to make it a championship building. Why couldn't we all come, even in our differences, to lay down the bricks of our stories with our differences as the mortar? Why couldn't you let us talk? Why couldn't you give us the platform so that we could have connected and motivated each other? Someone's story might have been the cement. Someone had the tools. Someone possessed this. Someone possessed that. Not everyone is going to be able to do the same job, but everyone can contribute. That's what gives a team the cutting edge. It's what gives the best chance at the championship.

Letter 18: Reflection

What stood out to you in this athlete's letter?

_____

_____

_____

_____

_____

If you were the athlete in this situation, how would you react to the coach if you had experienced all these things? What would you do to express your concerns?

_____

_____

_____

_____

If you were the coach in this situation, how would you respond to the athlete if this letter were written to you? Consider your initial reaction as well as any behavioral changes you might make.

_____

_____

_____

_____

LETTER
19

Dear Coach,

I can still hear you saying it, because you said it all the time: "I own you." Behind closed doors, you always reminded me how you didn't want me there. You made me well aware because of how many times you said it over and over again. You reminded me of how I made you look bad, which was always followed by telling me to quit. Sometimes you paired it with throwing equipment at me [in the training facility]. I know this [was] your defense mechanism, abusing us, because whenever we tried to talk to you about it, there wasn't really any dialogue. You would just shut us down.

Hear me out. I think there are two types of coaching mindsets. You have those coaches who are like, "What can I do to make these athletes successful in life, to be the best versions of themselves, and to reach their personal and professional goals?" Then you have those coaches who are like, "Okay, I am the coach. My goal is to become a coach at the highest level, and I am going to do whatever it takes to climb that ladder to achieve my goal." You were the latter. You made it clear to all of us, through how you treated us, that you only cared about yourself. You were doing it for the money, doing it for your name. It was always about what I could do for you, and if I couldn't help you reach your goals, then you didn't want to have anything to do with me.

After that first year is when I knew I needed to make some mental changes so I could survive you. When you started to go off the wall again, that is when I would picture myself as a ball, and anything you said to me would just bounce right back to you. I used it every single time we interacted. Interestingly enough, when I started to tune you out, that was my best year yet. I started doing a lot of self-coaching, a lot of self-motivation, which was about taking out the noise, even if the noise was put in my face. Every time you came at me, I reminded myself of what was most important. I would reset mentally. While it was my best athletic year yet, I was exhausted because I was so mentally drained from having to deal with you. To think about it now, I realize I could've put all that extra energy I was putting into managing my anger toward you into focusing on enjoying myself athletically, really just enjoying the process, as opposed to calming myself down because of you. I was focused on good things, but I subconsciously knew I was focused on them because you kept putting us in bad situations.

Even writing this letter, thinking about it again, my body feels tight. I feel that internal anger again because we didn't expect for it to be so miserable. While, yes, I grew from the experience, it was a painful growth—unnecessarily painful. There was no fun to it, no love or support—absolutely no support, which is ironic when you think about it. We had all those resources [elite athletic facilities] that made it look like we were supported, but in reality, we weren't. The real support would have happened if we felt emotionally, mentally, and physically supported by our inner circle, which included you, whether we liked it or not. Because to get the best out of your athletes, you needed to give us the best environment. You never gave us that. I was always perplexed as to why, even when I was giving you what you wanted: wins.

This is what I think it boiled down to: you had a lot of internal stuff going on. I think a lot of your anger stemmed from deep-rooted issues you experienced in your past, and you took that out on us. All that anger you had as a kid that you brought with you into adulthood trickled down to us. So, while I was so angry with you in the beginning, toward the end of my athletic career with you, I started to feel bad for you. It was clear that you really had no one who supported you. That is when I started to pray for you because everything that I didn't get from you, I started to realize, is everything that you didn't get from the world. You weren't given the best environment, or at least that's my best guess after putting all the puzzle pieces together over the years, so you weren't able to give us the best environment. I knew that, despite everything you'd done to me, I knew you needed help with your own internal demons because it was never me that did anything to you. You were just perceiving this world through an angry lens. You wanted something from the world. You felt the victim through a lot of your life, so you were always defensive with us.

I, too, like yourself, felt the victim for a while. Over time, though, I realized I wasn't going to follow in my family's footsteps. I wasn't going to follow their path. I wanted to live my own life and do my own things, so I made the choice not to be the victim anymore. I guess this is my way of giving you what I needed from you. What I wish I could have told you is this: I see you, and I am sorry. After I got past being victimized by you, I saw that you were just hurting. You just needed someone who cared, someone to be genuine and open with you. You don't deserve what happened to you. I hope you aren't hurting anymore. I hope you went to counseling and reconciled with your past because, at the end of the day, I just want what is best for you. We are family, and, as family, I wrote this letter because I care.

Letter 19: Reflection

What stood out to you in this athlete's letter?

_____

_____

_____

_____

If you were the athlete in this situation, how would you react to the coach if you had experienced all these things? What would you do to express your concerns?

_____

_____

_____

_____

If you were the coach in this situation, how would you respond to the athlete if this letter were written to you? Consider your initial reaction as well as any behavioral changes you might make.

_____

_____

_____

_____

LETTER 20

Dear Coach,

I struggle to even call you that anymore because I believe the title of "coach" is something you call someone when you respect and look up to them. Having you as a coach made me question everything that I did as an athlete and even made me question who I was as a person. But eventually I was freed from your demeaning coaching tactics, like when you showed my recruitment video to all the upper classmen and made fun of me before I even joined the team. Or when it was senior night and you had me stand up in front of all my teammates and parents while you poked fun at me for "not being good enough" and referencing the line from *Dumb and Dumber* to explain me and how I refused to accept failure: "So, you're telling me there's a chance." You made a joke of my hard work. By the end of my athletic career, I was left broken, depressed, stressed, and lost, wondering why I even played the sport to begin with. I was an athlete who loved my sport and was so passionate about it that your treatment of me even annoyed others because they couldn't understand. Sport was the one thing that truly made me happy. However, throughout my time with you as my coach, I slowly lost that feeling and dreaded nothing more than going to practice and being beaten down. I will never forget some of the comments that you said to me:

"You're only here because I need people on the team."

"You're not good enough, and I don't think you can be."

Here's one incident that sums up what kind of coach you are: You changed practice times for the spring season, which then made practice conflict with my work schedule, which I was unable to change. When I approached you one-on-one to discuss the issue, you said, "Well, you don't have to be on the team." I was shocked. You weren't even fazed by the fact that you just told one of your top players and captains to leave the team without even considering to help figure out a way that we could make this work. I left practice completely distraught and emotionally broken down. I didn't know what to do. I was lost, and the one person I should be able to go to for guidance was throwing me to the side like I was a piece of trash.

This was where you broke me. I couldn't fight back anymore. I was out of energy. I fell into a state of depression, quit my job to stay on the team, and went through the motions to finish my athletic career. Not only was I depressed but I was also angry. I hated you. You were supposed to be there for me, to support me, guide me. Instead, you beat me down. You made me hate the sport that I once loved because when I thought of the sport, I saw you. I lost all my identity, and it took me nearly a year to gain that back.

An athlete needs a coach who is going to lift them up and show them what kind of person they should be—not someone who is going to constantly put them down and diminish any kind of confidence they have. Coaches are mentors. They are people who challenge athletes to be the best that they can be, and they teach those athletes ways to take on adversities. You were not that. However, here's what I did learn from you: I learned that people deserve better. I deserved better. I learned how much of an impact a coach has on an athlete and how important your role as a coach is. You showed me all the things *not* to do and the consequences a coach's actions can have. A bad coach, like you, leads athletes to hate their sport, burn out, and perform poorly out of fear of failure or disappointing you. It can also lead to bad mental health (depression and anxiety). So, for that, I almost want to say thank you. You were not a good "coach"—if I can even call you that—but you still taught me valuable lessons. But at what cost? These methods of coaching are harmful to athletes. There are healthier ways of coaching that can produce the same valuable lessons of resilience and leave the athlete with a more positive experience. Coaches need to care for their athletes. They need to create a welcoming environment that the athletes want to be around. A coach is someone the athlete should be able to confide in when they are struggling. They are not someone who should create fear and discomfort. Finally, coaches need to listen to their athletes. Some of the best coaches learn the most when they actually take the time to hear what their athletes have to say.

Letter 20: Reflection

What stood out to you in this athlete's letter?

_____

_____

_____

_____

_____

If you were the athlete in this situation, how would you react to the coach if you had experienced all these things? What would you do to express your concerns?

_____

_____

_____

_____

If you were the coach in this situation, how would you respond to the athlete if this letter were written to you? Consider your initial reaction as well as any behavioral changes you might make.

_____

_____

_____

_____

LETTER
21

Dear Coach,

You tried to change me. You tried to break me. You tried to mold me to look like a champion—or at least your version of it: no emotion, a cool and collected player. Even if you didn't mean it, you tried to break me, and for a year or two, you succeeded. You had a way that you wanted your team to look and play. Athletically, I fit into that mold, but personality wise, I "had some work to do." You told me that I needed to have "the look of a champion," but you forced me to hide who I was, and you took away my form of expression. To you, the look of a champion was calm, cool, and collected, to show the same emotion whether winning or losing. A champion could not be, as you called it, "an emotional roller coaster," something you called me quite often.

But, Coach, to me, the *look of a champion* is passion. It is letting the pain of loss seep into your bones and motivate you for the next competition. The look of a champion, to me, is a player who radiates humility and confidence at the same time. A champion is someone who carries the emotion of their team when they are up and down. That was how I played at my best, with every emotion on my face. If I was confident and in my zone, everyone—including my opponent—knew it. Yes, they knew if I was down, but I also made sure to let them know when I was high, and when I'm at the highs, I take over. That was the player I was, the player that you would have gotten more out of. But that confidence vanished faster than I thought it ever could.

I wanted nothing more than to know why: Why you wanted me to conform so much to your vision of what a champion is "supposed" to be. Why it was so important that I stay in the box that you tried to put all of us in. You broke my spirit my first two years. If it wasn't for [my teammates], I would have been gone. Because of you, I lost the way I knew best how to play. All of my confidence was stripped, and instead of having a presence on the court, I became your average, go-through-the-motions player—something you were annoyed about but also it's what you created. I became the go-through-the-motions player because you stripped me of the very essence of who I was as an athlete.

I truly thought that if I worked harder than everyone every day, it would make a difference, but I was still a piece for you to move around and play with as you pleased. The end of my second year with you, you told me that after training for two completely different positions all year long, I would finally be a starter. You have no idea what that meant to me. After that meeting, I made the choice to not go home that summer. I stayed and worked hard every day. I worked harder than anyone in that weight room. I was in the gym at least three days a week working on my [technical and tactical skills]. My first year was going to be a statement to you that I deserved that spot. Turns out, that wasn't the case, though, was it?

Before our first preseason tournament, you decided that since one of the seniors was getting beat out in their position, you would move them to the right side. That senior was one of my closest friends, and you knew that. You pinned two friends against each other, trying to see which one of us could win your little mind game. Unfortunately for me, this spiked my anxiety, and as that grew, I began to fall into a depression for the second time in three years. My body was heavy all the time; practice was painful for me. Heck, even getting out of bed was hard, but like I said, I had something to prove to you. I wanted to make that statement, and friendship or not, you were going to know that you made the wrong choice.

Fast forward to the first quarter of the season. I had my chance, and I took it. For the next three games, I started and I excelled, but then it took a turn again. During an away game, I lost all sense of where I was, all balance, everything. Looking back, I don't remember coming out of the game, going into the locker room, the bus ride home, or how I even got back to my own house that night. That next morning, I woke up unable to move I was so weak. My roommate had to help me up and take me to urgent care to find out that I [was very sick]. I was devastated to find out that I would be out for at least four weeks.

When I told you, you acted like you didn't care, that it wasn't a big deal, and you told me that there probably wouldn't be a chance for me to play again the rest of the year. That pissed me off, but what pissed me off more was your surprise when, within two weeks, I was back on the court. I am not tooting my own horn when I admit that I worked harder than every single [athlete] on our team those next few weeks, trying to prove myself, but it was easy to see you had made up your mind. When I finally got the chance the second time, I had to hide the fact that I was so exhausted after every game that I would throw up for the first five minutes after, only to be told that *now* you wanted me to have more of a presence on the court, *now* you wanted me to have emotion, *now* you wanted my energy to run the team. When I practically had nothing to give, you demanded what you boxed up two years ago.

When I began playing for you, you imposed your definition of having "the look of a champion" to not only me but to the entire team as well. You drilled it into us that we shouldn't show emotion, that we should be cool and collected. Wanting to play so badly, I followed suit and gave in because that is what I believed would get me more playing time. But that mold that I was trying to fit into wasn't me. Who I am authentically is someone who shows emotion in everything they do. I feel the emotion and energy around me constantly, so for me, how you thought a champion should look is the exact opposite of what would have gotten you optimal performance out of me. What I needed from you was to nurture *my personal look of a champion*, which was that of showing the passion I had for the game and the hunger I had to succeed every second I was out there.

You were two years too late when you found that out—when you finally asked me to bring the energy, the emotion, the presence I had among the team. When you finally asked me to contribute that at the highest level possible, it was no surprise that I led our team for three games. The player you tried to hold back for an entire year helped you win three of our biggest games. It's what we could have accomplished together if you would have allowed me to be my authentic self from the start.

After that, I thought my last year with you would be different, but it wasn't. When I tried to be a leader, you made sure I knew my place. I was never given the title and was always ridiculed when I spoke up in the huddle, but my presence was still known throughout our conference. I made sure that, in spite of you, I was always the loudest and biggest presence. Our team was not a team without me, and once I noticed that, your game with my mind was done. This time I would win, and by the end of the season, I did. You had been so busy trying to break me that you didn't realize that I did everything in my power for my team so we could succeed.

Looking back, I didn't need a coach to try and mold me. I didn't need a coach to limit and contain me. I understand that you had a way you wanted your players to present themselves, and I respect that, but you didn't respect who I was. When you recruit someone with a loud personality and then you tell them to be composed, you are telling them to channel and hide who they are. You have to understand that everyone's "look of a champion" is different, and honestly, that is one of the first things you should have learned about your players. You had [athletes] coming from different towns, different states, different backgrounds, and you wanted them to all look the same, but all that was doing was teaching us how to be unquestionably obedient. Honestly, looking back, I think all I wanted was to be acknowledged and allowed to just flow with my own energy—whether I was a "roller coaster of emotions" or not. In the four years that I played for you, it took you until our banquet to admit the gym would not be the same without my spirit in it. That was all I wanted to be acknowledged for, as the leader and asset to our team that I was. I wanted to play with the emotion of a champion, not the look of a champion, because it's the heart of an athlete, not just the look, that can get us the performance outcomes we want. I truly wonder where I would have been if you would not have limited me.

Letter 21: Reflection

What stood out to you in this athlete's letter?

_____

_____

_____

_____

_____

If you were the athlete in this situation, how would you react to the coach if you had experienced all these things? What would you do to express your concerns?

_____

_____

_____

_____

If you were the coach in this situation, how would you respond to the athlete if this letter were written to you? Consider your initial reaction as well as any behavioral changes you might make.

_____

_____

_____

_____

_____

LETTER
22

Dear Coach,

I am so happy that I didn't let you make me hate the sport I am so passionate about, all those years ago. I am now a head coach. How does that make you feel? Knowing you, you'll take full advantage of that and say that you taught me everything I know. You did teach me what *not* to do, so thank you for that. You thought I would never amount to anything; you made that painfully clear. Because of you, I wanted to become a coach so that I could give players a much better experience than the one I had for those three years.

First Year

Do you remember when I went into your office asking if you knew my [sibling]? I didn't know they yelled and talked back to you at the other [organization]. Is that where the target on my back started, or was it something I did? Hopefully, one day, I will have enough guts to ask you in person. I really want to know. Maybe it could be a growing point for me as well because I have gone through those three years over and over and over again in my head to try and figure it out.

I was so excited to be on your team. I looked up to you and the team so much. Conditioning started in August. I never missed one, even though they were optional. I would have done anything for that team. Tryouts came around; my [sibling] was also trying out. You put us toward each other in a one versus one. Why? Looking back now, that would be awesome in normal practice, but not during tryouts when the pressure is already on. I beat [my sibling], of course, but my [my sibling] still says, to this day, that they let me win. Yeah, right. My catching wasn't the best that day, I know that. You put me on JV. I was the fastest, hardest worker out there, by a stretch. But you are the coach, so I didn't question your judgment. Like any good athlete, I respected your decision.

JV was fine. We worked hard with our assistant coach, who was really just our school's cheerleading coach; I guess you were that desperate to find someone to help. It was hard for us as athletes to take the cheerleading coach seriously at first. They didn't even do their homework to learn the game or at least try. All they knew was how to make us run and learn how to catch. Let's just say, though, my catching was near perfect, and I was in great shape. Summer rolled around, and I went to a camp, which you suggested. It was pretty good; I learned a lot. I was ready to make varsity the next year.

Second Year

August rolled around, and conditioning started again. I never missed one. Other people missed all the time, for one excuse or another, but you could always depend on me to be there. I also didn't want that to be a reason you put me on JV again, because you didn't think I was dedicated enough. Tryouts came. I had a great tryout, and I thought I made varsity for sure.

I confidently walked over to the paper hanging in the courtyard. I just knew I made it. My parents taught me to always work hard, and that was finally paying off. I checked the paper; my name wasn't there. All those people who missed conditioning and were lazy, who didn't practice on their own, and who were not as fast as me—the list goes on—they made varsity. I was crushed. That was all I wanted. I put the work in. Hard work always equals results, right? That was a hard lesson that you taught me: that my best, which was better than others, wasn't enough.

I went into your office to talk to you about it. You said, "You must be mad at me, huh?" I told you I wasn't (lying, of course) and that I just wanted to know what I could work on to make varsity next year. You said playing with my left hand: if I could play better with my left hand the next couple of games, you would give me the opportunity to move up. I was so excited. I raced home and worked on my left hand for the next week. Now, normally, I would average at least nine goals a game. This game, I only had five, but they were all left-handed shots. I ran up to you, so excited, to see what you had to say. I asked you if you saw my goals. You said no, that you weren't paying attention. I went back to my team, trying to hold the tears in. What was I doing wrong?

That's when the thoughts started to pop in: I wanted to transfer from your team to another. I wanted to get out of there. This was my passion! I tried everything! We won the championship that year. We were so excited to win that one of my teammates peed their pants the day we won because, against all odds, we beat a team we had never beaten before. I was nominated as [position] of the year. But none of it mattered—or at least to you anyway. What I learned is this: it didn't matter how I viewed my achievements (by the way, they meant the world to me). What I learned is that my achievements were only considered worthy if *you* considered them worthy. What I learned is that my worth isn't dictated by my definition of worth but through the eyes of external others. You stole the joy of every single one of those achieving moments from me because you defined them as "not enough."

My parents were livid, but they always believed in us advocating for ourselves. Instead of getting angry at you, we found the best [sport] camp there was in the whole nation to send me to. They won nationals the last four years. I traveled by myself up to that camp and got to play with the most elite players in the nation for that week. I learned so much, so I was excited to see how well third year was going to go for me.

Third Year

Conditioning started, and I, of course, never missed one. Not only did I not miss a conditioning, but I also pushed myself even more than the year before. No one was going to out-work me. I was determined to not let you look past me. I was quieter that year; I felt different. I ran before conditioning practice and after I got home, listening to my music and crying. I hated you. I had too much respect because of the lessons my parents supported me through to ever say anything to you about it. I questioned, *Was I not cut out for [this sport]? Was my gut feeling of passion wrong for [this sport]?* I felt so lost. I really, really tried to get my parents to let me transfer, but they said it was a good life lesson to sort through this. They weren't wrong, but that is not what I wanted to hear. Then, tryouts came around. I was so nervous. This was it for me. If I didn't make varsity this year, I was going to be done. JV wasn't challenging me enough. I knew I needed something more.

I left the tryout feeling numb—I don't even remember what I thought about it. The next day, I anxiously walked up to that piece of paper in the courtyard. Finally, my name was under varsity. Finally, my hard work paid off. That's when you changed toward me. When I finally made it that year, you were nice to me. Was that a motivation tactic to try and make me better, being so unkind to me for the first two years? Did you think that tactic was going to motivate me? Here's what you need to know: it's what caused my depression. You continued to have your favorites; I knew that part wasn't going to change. So, I wasn't surprised when I saw you recently and you said that one particular player was your "favorite." I hope you don't display that like you did back in my time.

As a coach now, I think everyone has favorites. The problem about how you did things is that you made it blatantly clear that two [athletes] on our team were your favorites. It made the rest of us feel like we weren't good enough, and no matter what we did, we wouldn't be good enough. I am a different person than everyone else. It made me work harder to try and get to that level where I might one day be a favorite of yours, but I always fell short because you made that level an impossible goal. The other [athletes] on the team? They tried less; they got lazy; they didn't see a point. I wish you would have seen it, or maybe you did and didn't care.

The season went fine. You moved me down to defense. I was so mad. I was always such a strong player in my position. I was devastated. Was nothing I did good enough? I was one of the fastest on my team, so why not keep me in [this particular position] where my speed could better be used? Instead of working with me on what needed to be changed, you just turned my whole world upside down. You did something new that year, a "highly suggested" spring break trip. I went, while those same great people who didn't show up to conditioning had better plans.

We made it to the semifinals in the playoffs. An [athlete] from the other team flicked you off. Word must travel fast about what a peach you were/are. We lost by one goal. You told us, going into next year, that the spring break trip was mandatory. I told you I already had a trip planned to see family and to go see some schools I applied to. You told me, "I guess you aren't trying out then." Again. How could you break my heart *again*? I thought it wasn't possible. I tried again to talk my parents into letting me transfer. They wouldn't allow it. They told me to find something else to do. So I played another sport in fall. It was fun but not my sport.

Today

Having since moved away, I asked one of my friends, who knows you, about you. They said, "Let's just say [coach] is not high on everyone's Christmas list." That made me sad for you. You must be so lonely. I wonder how much your life would change if you were more caring, compassionate, and empathetic. I really do feel for you and hope that you can change someday—not only for the countless lives that you influence but for yourself. Being the way you are must keep you up at night (or maybe not). I was at an airport and saw a [person] with [our old] logo written on their shirt. I said, "Wow, I used to play there!" The [parent] then said, "Did you have the same coach? My child just quit because of the way [the coach] treated them. It was a shame because they really loved the sport." I told [the parent] what I was doing now and to please not let [their child] quit the game they love.

As mentioned, I am a head coach now. I present to coaches about team culture, being a caring coach, which means caring about more than just [the Xs and Os] with the athletes. My passion, which matters to me more than anything else in this world, has led me to travel all over the country spreading the word on positive coaching and how much it can change the way athletes feel about themselves and about their team. Each time I am in front of a training group, I think about you. I wish you would have attended a positive training or even paid more attention to what you were doing, not just to me but to the rest of the team. I love what I do because of the athletes I work with and the *relationship* we have built together. That's the key: the relationship. Something that I never had as your athlete but secretly I craved. I wanted so badly to be noticed by you that I went to great lengths to get it. Looking back, I caused myself so much heartache and depression trying to be what you wanted me to be. What I realize now is that no one was ever going to accomplish that because you didn't see your own worth in yourself. So how could you have seen it in others?

Every year, I receive a couple of emails from coaches thanking me for what they learned during my training. They tell me how much their team has changed and how much better they play. Now, the unity on the team is unmatched, and the team works together toward a common goal. The culture they instilled in their team is actually helping their game out; the athletes are being positive and not putting each other down. Imagine if you implemented just a couple of positive things how much better your team would be. But don't just take my word for it. Here is one excerpt from an email I received from a coach after they attended these positive coaching clinics (and basically learned how to be everything you were not):

I'll keep this short by [sharing] a quick story about our team. Last summer, we lost every single game and got absolutely crushed in each. This spring, we won five of our seven regular season games to finish tied for the top position. In the season-ending playoffs this past weekend, we won the championship! I'd love to take all of the credit for the amazing turnaround, but I know I played just a tiny role, if any, in the results. You certainly played a role in our success as I attempted to implement as many [of the positive coaching] things as I could remember from the clinic. Thank you!

You taught me what not to do, which is what has led me to where I am today: spreading the word of positive coaching and the fantastic effect it has on athletes and their mental space. Being a positive coach is as easy as pointing out what the athlete does well, not just their mistakes. It is not yelling at them each time they miss a pass or don't quite get to where they need to be in time. It is about being patient and supportive as these kids work through what they should be doing. Ask your athlete how their day is going. You might be surprised to hear what they are going through; this life can be cruel. When you take a positive approach, it allows athletes to not be scared to make a mistake. If you coach by fear, motivation will run out. If you coach by positivity and caring, that player will work harder for you because of the support you gave them. They feel better about themselves and allow themselves to show more effort. Nothing is better than that!

That's what we, as coaches, need to care about. We have a responsibility to these athletes to not only teach them the sport but also to provide them a safe space where they know they are cared for, loved, and acknowledged. While lessons can still be taught when you coach like you coach, please understand the earth-shattering effects that, even as an adult, still bring painful tears to my eyes. What we need to know is this: more powerful lessons can be taught when we, as coaches, empathetically show up for these athletes.

Letter 22: Reflection

What stood out to you in this athlete's letter?

_____

_____

_____

_____

_____

If you were the athlete in this situation, how would you react to the coach if you had experienced all these things? What would you do to express your concerns?

_____

_____

_____

_____

If you were the coach in this situation, how would you respond to the athlete if this letter were written to you? Consider your initial reaction as well as any behavioral changes you might make.

_____

_____

_____

_____

_____

LETTER
23

Dear Coach,

"The opposite of right is not wrong. It's left. A coach's job is not to criticize but to redirect."

I ran into this quote a couple of weeks ago on Twitter. The person who posted it is also a coach. They had some great insights that really got me thinking about how to be a good coach, which is the opposite of everything you were.

I remember wanting to be a part of your program because of the success it had. I had seen video interviews with you and different team members from different years. They all had one thing in common: the athletes spoke very highly of you. You talked a good game about how you invested yourself in every athlete from the national champion contender to the walk-on wanting to have a change in their athletic career. My previous institution also spoke highly of you, not just as a coach but a person. I had full faith in my previous coach and looked forward to making you my new coach. At the same time, I wanted to come to your program because of the continued success of your athletes and program altogether. I must say, I was bitterly disappointed, not just in you but in the team environment you instigated.

Coming into the program, I was a walk-on, which automatically isn't as respected as a recruit, much less a top recruit. However, you talked a good game about how you cared about every athlete on the team. Despite the fact you said this, I didn't expect to be seen much or treated highly. I did, however, expect for myself and my efforts to be respected—a basic standard of human decency. I never approached you because you were either "too busy" or all of your attention was focused on the top athletes. With that, you entirely disregarded athletes like me. Again, I didn't think much of it at first. I understood you had a lot of pressure on you to try and get the teams prepped to defend the national titles. I went on to kind of do my own thing and do a little experimenting in training to see what could work for me with the new training program. Things didn't go so hot for me, but I wasn't too worried. I knew what I was capable of, so I just adjusted and moved on.

However, once we got to the next season, I tried approaching you more as it was my first time in this environment; I didn't want my first impression of you to ruin how I interacted with you the rest of the time we were together. I wanted advice and guidance on what you thought would be best for me, but you still never made time for me or had any intention of guiding me. Again, I just washed it away. I went on to do my own thing again and essentially became my own coach. I made the choice to compete in a certain way, but after an unsuccessful season, I wanted to shift focus and compete differently for the next season. When I told you that, you hardly paid attention to it. You just said, "Okay," and turned your back on me. My first year, my [competitions were] few as I had to pay my own way. You never made an effort to help me find good competitions, much less to prep myself in a way that I could really put myself out there.

Sadly, I ended my season early and shifted my focus to my first season in the jersey I was so excited to wear. However, the same trend continued. You showed no respect for me as an athlete, and worst of all, you showed no respect to me as a person. I never sought your attention or approval. I noticed many athletes on the team would suck up to you just so they could be seen and noticed by you. I wanted you to notice me based on my efforts and commitment to the team and the training, not because I was sucking up. All while being a full-time student, I also had a part-time job. I worked the night shifts and, as a consequence, would not get the sleep I needed. It wasn't ideal, but it's what I had to do to make ends meet. Even so, I was still able to keep up with many of the top athletes. You knew I had a job but still paid no respect to me or my hard work.

It only got worse. At our second competition of the season, I competed exactly how you asked of me. You asked me to put myself out there and not let fear determine how I competed. I did this, but I still was only slightly beat out by another athlete. When it came to picking the travel team for the next competition, you didn't choose me. I didn't have the outcome you wanted, but process wise, I did everything you asked of me. You didn't care about that. You failed to see that I was still fairly new in this environment, so it would likely take a couple of attempts for me to obtain the desired results. Although I was frustrated, I moved on from it and focused on the next competition. I felt that you stole a great chance from me to truly prove myself.

As the season progressed, you shifted practices to the afternoon due to the cold weather. I told you I would still have to train in the morning because I had other obligations in the afternoon. I couldn't quit my job as my roommates stuck their necks out to help me get this job so I could help my parents with the rent, bills, and groceries. You didn't seem to care and ultimately paid even less attention to me—if getting less attention from you was even possible. Every time I walked by you, you would turn your head the other way and completely ignore me. One time you even told me that there was no reason I should be working. I wanted to talk back to you really badly! I bit my tongue out of respect. It was clear to me that you didn't understand why I had to work.

You made a post on Twitter earlier in the season where you expressed how "proud and honored you were" to coach a team that was so diverse in upbringings, ethnicities, traditions, and other demographics. All that was BS in my eyes. You only paid attention to the white athletes, the Australian, Irish, and English athletes, probably because you yourself are white. So I question how you can be "proud and honored" to coach such a diverse team. You never even tried to get to know the diversity on your team. We were simply poster children for you so that you could parade around and act like you were an example of diversity and inclusion. Don't disrespect me like that. While the white athletes might have been considered the top athletes, you still never gave any of the rest of us a chance. Because I was not white, you made me feel less than, which was another way you ignored my talents. So, I continued doing what I was doing. I coached myself. I got results, but it would have been really nice if you would have been there for me, not just as a coach but as an advocate, a champion, a decent human being.

You are by far the worst coach I have ever known. The team environment was just as toxic as your mindset. The team was full of phony sycophantic suck-ups, and you welcomed it because it fed your ego. If an athlete didn't try to suck up to you, you just brushed them to the side, regardless of how hard they worked. The team was the same. I myself acted as I always have: focused, with very few words, just doing what I had to do. The others realized that I wasn't worried about fitting in or being fake or talking behind other athletes' backs; so, as you did, they immediately ostracized me. It definitely made competing for a horrible team extremely hard. However, I came with a purpose, with goals, and I didn't plan on letting anything get in the way of that. I was a resilient person before I even came into your program, so that's what I used to deal with you. While I knew I was able to come back stronger from everything you caused me, I can only imagine how much more I would have been able to accomplish if you hadn't been so horrible. Yes, I am stronger mentally, emotionally, and physically—because of my own doing—but at what expense? I spent years feeling worthless because of you. The only thing I learned from you was what type of coach I shouldn't be.

Although you made me feel awful a lot and made me feel like I was worthless, I used that to my advantage to make myself stronger as an athlete and, most important, as a person. You only cared about winning. That's why you had a team full of people who had no integrity. You didn't bother developing your athletes to be good people, and that's why the environment was highly toxic. You showed me what it is like to be a horrible coach and what type of coach I should not be. Knowing what I know now, this is what I needed from you. I needed you to cut the BS and, first and foremost, acknowledge me as a human being, not just as a machine. Yes, I came to compete, but I am more than just the outcomes I can produce for you. There are so many things about me—my background, my heritage, my upbringing—that you could have connected with. If you would have connected with me in those ways, I would have felt invincible. I would not have felt so alone through the whole process, which would have helped me perform a little better. It also would have been nice if you had been a coach who championed diversity and inclusion. Cut the tweets and walk the talk. I needed you to not just favor the white athletes but favor us all. That would have helped create a less toxic team environment where we could have felt more unified, and a unified team is a stronger team, both physically and mentally.

Letter 23: Reflection

What stood out to you in this athlete's letter?

_____

_____

_____

_____

_____

If you were the athlete in this situation, how would you react to the coach if you had experienced all these things? What would you do to express your concerns?

_____

_____

_____

_____

If you were the coach in this situation, how would you respond to the athlete if this letter were written to you? Consider your initial reaction as well as any behavioral changes you might make.

_____

_____

_____

_____

_____

LETTER
24

Dear Coach,

I am writing this letter to inform you of all the things I didn't
have the courage to tell you in person. As a young athlete, multiple
years before I joined your team, I had an unfortunate athletic experience due to a verbally and emotionally abusive coach. The coach
would tell my teammates and I that we had "loser" and "idiot"
written all over our foreheads. The coach's actions and words took
a negative toll on both my athletic performance and overall mentality. I started to be less energetic, more careless, depressed, and I
lost all confidence in myself. I began to go down in my level of play
and started becoming a weak athlete. I lost my love of the game
after that experience. I thought my athletic career was over after
that, but I decided to move on and continue playing. It was one of
my best decisions.

Fortunately for me, my new coach really gave the love of the
game back to me. The amount of passion, positivity, encouragement, and well-rounded coach-athlete relationship inspired me to
keep playing. This coach's coaching style was virtue based, and I
learned not only athletic skills but life skills as well. Some of the
virtues this coach promoted were fairness, responsibility, integrity,

compassion, respect, positivity, and the shaping of our character. Their coaching style influenced my sport performance and overall mental health in a positive manner. They helped to develop in me an overall positive and strong mentality through any situation, and it led my athletic performance to excel. Their style of operant learning was through positivity. My experience was so memorable that I thought the right choice was to continue to play on your team. Well, I was wrong.

I was happy to continue pursuing my athletic career, which caused me to set my standards way too high and have higher hopes than I should have. When I first met you, I thought you were going to be a great coach based on your personality outside of the sport, but you proved me wrong. Your style of coaching is something that I have never experienced before. I never thought it could get any worse than the verbally and emotionally abusive coach I had as a child, but it did. I was accepting verbal and emotional abuse from you just because I thought that's what I was supposed to do. Not only did this create short-term damage [in sport], it created long-term damage in my life. Your way of coaching really affected my life outside of sport. You caused me to experience depression, something that I never thought possible in something I loved. It influenced almost all aspects of my life, including school, work, and relationships. I was sad all the time and felt worthless. This unfortunately caused me to be angry, on edge all the time, and negative. I felt that way because of what I experienced from you every day; I took it out on the ones that I love the most. It also caused me to be less attentive in school, which is something I am so passionate about.

All the yelling, storming off, sighs, comments, and hidden messages, such as eye rolling, affected me more than I thought. I am very responsive to positive feedback and constructive criticism, but your way of coaching was all negative and demeaning. Each time you would show any type of negativity, my mental state declined. My actions began to reflect your way of coaching in the way that I would just be so negative to myself and give up. I tend to be a fairly positive, happy individual, but since I was around a coach like you, who was so negative, I began to lose my authenticity, which negatively influenced me in so many ways (e.g., sport performance, mental health). All you do is yell and expect perfection. You didn't even give the effort to try and coach our team. If we weren't winning, which was usually the case, you turned against us. You made me not want to put the work in because I saw that you had given up. I didn't want to play for you, and I didn't think you deserved to have me on your team. I felt as if I was wasting my time playing for you. I was miserable every single day. After all that, your style of coaching was abandonment—you literally stopped holding practices.

I would have never expected any coach to not want to practice, especially at our level of play. Your style of coaching was so lazy. Not only was my mental state going downhill but my physical ability to play was as well. My level of play dropped dramatically, and I didn't have those fundamentals anymore. It really got in my head as my performance began to decline. You didn't care. You didn't care to practice or coach. You expected us to be perfect. You said, "If you think you need practice by now at this level, then you shouldn't be here." I couldn't believe it when I heard you say that, but I began to believe it when I realized that we would only practice about two days of the week for thirty minutes each. Half of the time, you weren't even there and that really showed me that you didn't care. I was not able to practice fully until my [parent] came to help me. I got more practice and coaching from my [parent] twice a week for a month when they were here than I did all year from you. Not being able to perform to the best of my ability due to lack of practice caused me to lose all confidence in myself.

I dreaded going to practice and playing in games because you made me lose all confidence in myself. I would call home almost every week and just cry to my parents because of how bad my experience was because of you. I didn't have the strength mentally to ignore your actions. I didn't know how not to let your behaviors affect me. Some might read this and think I'm not cut out for sport. Some might think I should have been strong enough to ignore your actions and just play. How sad is that, though? Where's the accountability? Are we just supposed to ignore your behaviors that led to my depression? This was supposed to be my second place away from home, but you ruined that. A coach to me is someone who is a role model or a second parent, just because we spend so much time with them. They're someone who is positive, encouraging, passionate, knowledgeable, mature, and caring. None of that describes you. It felt like the longest season of my life, but somehow, I got through it because I'm resilient.

You caused me pain and depression that not only influenced my athletic performance but my overall mentality as well. You gave me negativity by yelling, ignoring, throwing things, eye rolling, and giving up. What I needed was positivity and encouragement. You ruined my mental state by your verbally, emotionally, and physically abusive ways. What I needed from you was maturity. You demeaned me. What I needed from you was care. You ignored our team when we needed you most. What we needed from you was unconditional passion toward the game, no matter the win/loss record. What I needed—what we all needed—was a knowledgeable coach who would refuse to be a fair-weather fan. What we needed is what we deserved.

Letter 24: Reflection

What stood out to you in this athlete's letter?

_____

_____

_____

_____

_____

If you were the athlete in this situation, how would you react to the coach? What would you do to express your concerns?

_____

_____

_____

_____

If you were the coach in this situation, how would you respond to the athlete if this letter were written to you? Consider your initial reaction as well as any behavioral changes you might make.

_____

_____

_____

_____

_____

_____

LETTER
25

Dear Coach,

Well, it's been a while since we have talked. I think we bumped into each other once at a meet a few years after I graduated, but that may have been the only time we have talked since I graduated so long ago. You know I became a coach, right? We should have had a lot to talk about, a good reason to keep in touch, right? I wonder if you kept in touch with anyone else from the team. I doubt it.

When I look back on the four years we spent almost every day together, I always say that my relationship with you was "fine." On the technical side, you made me the [athlete] I became. The attention to detail you ingrained in me became a quest for continual improvement and excellence. Your voice was always in my ear (and it never went out the other ear), and because of that, I think I became one of those rare [athletes] who improved consistently in college. I give you so much credit for the fact that I was [performing at my best] at my final championship [competition], turning me into an All-American and school record holder.

So, with what I consider to be a very successful collegiate career, why were things between us just "fine"? Maybe it was because you were such a great technician, but you didn't value other parts of the coaching game. There was something missing on the personal side. I can't remember ever going into your office before or after practice just to chat. I don't remember you being at graduation. I never sought you out for advice outside of sport. When I eventually made my decision to pursue coaching as a career, I called on a few coaching mentors. I did not call you.

And although you were not a coaching mentor to me, I found myself modeling much of my early coaching off of you. I did much of what you did. I used a lot of your drills and sets. I demanded perfection from my athletes. If a mistake was made, we redid it. I yelled from time to time, probably not as much as you did, though. I gave punishments like you—twenty minutes of burpees for an athlete who was late to practice. I was hard, and my athletes always worked hard, just like yours. They also were successful, just like yours.

But my coaching style evolved. I eventually became more like "me" and less like "you." I quit yelling. Yelling has never been authentic to me; it felt like I was putting on an act. My athletes frequented my office just to pass time. I went to my athletes' graduation. Rather than punishments, I usually just had a conversation with my athletes. A few of them even came over for Thanksgiving dinner when they decided not to make the trip home.

I look back over my first few years in coaching somewhat regretfully because I wasn't a softer place to land for some of my athletes. I don't blame you, Coach. I just wasn't aware of how much your style of coaching rubbed off on me. I hope you are well and wish the best for you, and maybe the next time we run into each other, I will ask you to join me for a drink.

Letter 25: Reflection

What stood out to you in this athlete's letter?

_____

_____

_____

_____

If you were the athlete in this situation, how would you react to the coach if you had experienced all these things? What would you do to express your concerns?

_____

_____

_____

_____

If you were the coach in this situation, how would you respond to the athlete if this letter were written to you? Consider your initial reaction as well as any behavioral changes you might make.

_____

_____

_____

_____

LETTER
26

Dear Coach (and any other coach out there who has lost touch with why they started coaching in the first place),

You wanted us to handle the responsibilities of an adult, but you treated us like children. You felt like you had to lie to us about playing time, what our role was, and how we were doing, just so you could keep us somewhat happy when we realized you were not going to play us. Let me let you know something, Coach. We are not as out of touch with reality as you think. We are not stupid. You sugarcoating everything that you said to us just made us label you as a liar, as not genuine. We are adults, so please be as straight up as you can with your future athletes. It will at least make us feel like you care enough to tell us what we need to do to get better and that you respect us and love us enough to be real with us. But that was not the case. It made us feel like we did not exist and were unimportant in your eyes. You treated us like kids but wanted us to act like adults. I needed you to be real. Be honest. Be upfront. You are only hurting your athletes by lying to them. Sometimes you would just completely avoid any conversations that could lead to conflict. You would just blow us off because it was a conversation that you did not want to have. How is that fair?

I understand better than most that you cannot coach all athletes the same. Every single one is different and motivated by different things. But you can hold every single person to the same standards, especially off the floor. You made it too obvious who you did not like, Coach. Honestly, I have never been mistreated, in my opinion, but someone very close to me on the team had been constantly walked on and disrespected just because you thought you were better than [this athlete]. And that was detrimental to every single player's view toward you. You wanted us to be family, so how you treated one player is how you treated all of us. You lose respect when you mistreat your athletes. When you lose our respect, Coach, then we lose our motivation to play hard for you.

I am the type of player who will give you everything I have, no matter what, but most players are not like that. You have to build and sustain that positive relationship; otherwise, there is no way the athlete will reach their full potential. If I was not so worried about our relationship and how that affected me, then I could have played so much better on a more consistent basis. I could not, though. It is sad, honestly, because you almost start wishing your team would lose so that your coach wouldn't get the satisfaction of a win. Be more conscious of what you say and to whom. We hear everything that you say to us. We take it to heart, so be more careful. I know you say it is not personal, but a lot of times, it is, and a lot of times, coaches are the ones who make it personal. Think about what you are going to say and then put yourself in your player's shoes and try to understand how they would respond to it.

In my opinion, you had the opportunity to change lives. I don't know if the money or the pressure got to you and you changed, but you did not change our lives. You did not make a positive impact. You did not make us feel loved or important or bright.

Once you break our trust once, it is almost impossible to get it back. We all talk. What you tell one athlete, you tell the whole team usually. So why would you think that it's okay to tell one of us one thing and then go tell me something completely different? If you think I am going to trust a coach over a teammate who is supposed to be my "family," then you are lost.

You kicked my best friend off the team in a nine-minute meeting—a kid you knew had been through it. [This athlete] dealt with so much over their life, with one of those being how mistreated they were by their last coach. You knew that, but you did not try to get to know [this athlete]. You did not try to help them. You kept giving them just enough hope so that they would not cause problems, and then you just axed them.

A coach can have such a huge impact on a kid. I have seen it firsthand, positively and negatively. You could change people's lives just by acting like you loved and believed in them, but you struggled to do that. Be genuine. Discover again why you started coaching in the first place. I see you and many other coaches, and I get terrified that one day I will end up like you. In my experience with college coaches, it seems like they lose their "why." Every coach I have ever met started coaching because they wanted to make a positive impact on young athletes' lives or something of the sort. But over time, it is like they forget this purpose and shift toward putting money, glory, wins, and themselves first. I am scared that I will one day make it more about the money than the kids, that I will lose touch with my purpose and compassionate side. It seems like it happens to so many coaches; it's disappointing. I know we make mistakes. When we are players, we think that the coaches shouldn't [make mistakes], but coaches are human, too. There is no excuse for not loving your players, for not treating them with the respect and compassion that they deserve.

Coach, think about what you do before you do it. Think about what you say before you say it. And most important, think about how your athletes are going to perceive your words and actions. Perception is reality. Be kind, compassionate, and understanding. Empower us. Make us feel valued. If you do those things, then I think you can get almost any kid to run through a wall for you.

I'll leave you with a few quotes I want you to think about:

> *"The interesting thing about coaching is that you have to trouble the comfortable and comfort the troubled."*
> —Ric Charlesworth

> *"A common mistake among those who work in sport is spending a disproportional amount of time on Xs and Os as compared to time spent learning about people."*
> —Mike Krzyzewski

> *"I'd say handling people is the most important thing you can do as a coach. I've found every time I've gotten into trouble with a player, it's because I wasn't talking to them enough."*
> —Lou Holtz

Remember, please, making a positive impact on a kid's life is what will lead to more wins. I think you were confused and thought it was the other way around.

Letter 26: Reflection

What stood out to you in this athlete's letter?

_____

_____

_____

_____

_____

If you were the athlete in this situation, how would you react to the coach if you had experienced all these things? What would you do to express your concerns?

_____

_____

_____

_____

If you were the coach in this situation, how would you respond to the athlete if this letter were written to you? Consider your initial reaction as well as any behavioral changes you might make.

_____

_____

_____

_____

_____

LETTER 27

Dear Coach,

I wish I didn't feel such a strong urge to write this letter. Before I put pen to paper, however, I had to take time to reflect and investigate that feeling further. It's taken time, and it was difficult to put my finger on what exactly I'd want to say to you, so I'll just share a bit about why I felt the urge to share.

Maybe it's simply because you came at the end of a long line of less-than-extraordinary coaches. I could have just had some bad luck when it came to coaches, and maybe you had some bad luck, too. [Maybe it's because] you came last in the line for me, or maybe it's because you even had less-than-extraordinary coaches so you were just doing your best with the worst you were given. Here I am, rationalizing again to try to make sense of it all because it's got to be more than that; otherwise, I wouldn't feel the urge to write this.

Maybe it's because you showed us it wasn't okay to make a mistake. You would tell us that you wanted us to try new things, be creative, and take chances, but if it didn't come off, then you would get mad. You would take us out when we made a bad pass or stop practice if we lost the ball. I feel like you probably know this already, but I wish you truly knew what it looked like in practice. Mistakes are how we grow, Coach. After all, how else can we learn? All we learned was how to avoid getting taken out of a game, which stunted the creativity I needed in order to take my game to the next level.

It's probably because you didn't practice what you preached. One of your big values was being on time. How do you expect us to respect you if, for example, I still have multiple texts on my phone from you asking me to let the team know that you were going to be late? I wish you modeled what it looked like to live up to one of the expectations you had set for us. I can't tell you how many times I fielded the question from my teammates, "How come Coach can be late, but I can't?" You put me in a rough spot, Coach. It wasn't fair to me or the rest of the team. My desire to show up every day and give maximum effort diminished because I lost respect for you. I wasn't present at practice. My mind was elsewhere because I wanted to be elsewhere, and that affected my effort and, ultimately, my performance on the field.

Maybe it's because of the guilt I feel toward our assistant coach. I feel like I let them down. When the athletic director came to us and asked if the assistant coach was head coach material, you know what I said? I said, "They are great in the role they are in now. We love the assistant coach, but I don't think they are ready to be a head coach." Oh, boy, was I wrong. I still carry that guilt a few years later. I feel like I let the team down by shifting my trust to you. I mean, what else was I supposed to do? You were the head coach, so you must know what you're doing. That title carries weight and expectations, and I blindly trusted you at first, hoping you would live up to it. Now, I don't even like to call you "coach."

Maybe it's because I could've used some of that trust from you. I needed you to trust us, Coach. We ran things without a coach for five months before you got there. We established a team that was actually a cohesive unit, one that found joy in the work and made it a point to find time to practice our craft because it was fun. It was fun to go play pickup and compete, but then it stopped. It was clear to see that you didn't trust in me; you didn't trust in us. We had put so much work into our team, and you didn't even acknowledge that. You didn't take the time to observe and assess the situation, to get to know us. You wanted to jump in and assert your dominance. How'd you do that? By trying to make mandatory practice sessions behind closed doors where you would come and run them (an [organizational] violation, cough, cough), and you expected me to go along with it. What you didn't care to see was that everyone was already showing up to our voluntary pickups anyways. The fact that I'm having to sit here and type a letter discussing the written and unwritten rules of the game—the athlete shouldn't have to coach the coach.

Maybe it's because I needed feedback from you. I wanted to get better. I would come into your office and try and check in about how things were going. I would ask, "What else should I be doing? How do you think I can improve my game to help the team?" You would just brush it off and say, "You're fine." I wasn't fine. I wasn't the best player I could be. I was craving coaching. If anything, I feel like that's one thing coaches should be good at: providing technical feedback. I wanted (and honestly needed) someone other than the voice in my head to provide honest, direct feedback. It's challenging when the only feedback you get is from the critic inside your head. When a coach leaves an athlete vulnerable to their internal critic, usually outcomes are not the best. Because you didn't help intercept the voice in my head, I felt at the mercy of my own thoughts. I would tell myself, "Oh, man, you suck. That was a stupid decision." Or even ask myself, "Dang . . . do I deserve to be playing at this level?" These are the thoughts I was having about my athletic performance, and if there's one thing I've learned, it's that this type of thinking is not conducive to performing at a high level. Coaches need to care about the mental aspect of the game. So, while you probably think it was my fault for not getting better, you really need to take a look in the mirror. Athletes need honest feedback from their coaches. It helps us see ourselves in a real, positive light. We want to know what we need to work on and also know that you see what we are bringing to the table. Help us by validating our worth as an athlete and, when appropriate, as a human being. Your lack of feedback heavily influenced my athletic performance. You fueled my internal critic, which left me feeling hopeless.

Maybe it's because you made inappropriate comments about our teammate's [sibling]. Ones that I, quite frankly, don't feel comfortable repeating. All I will say is this: sexism in any way, shape, or form is never okay! You crossed the line, and I should have called you on it in the moment. Looking back, I wonder why I didn't call you on it right when you said it. Probably because of the attitude of fear you instilled in most of us. I didn't feel safe to call you out because I knew you would passively punish me by cutting my playing time or ostracizing me altogether.

Last, and probably most dear to me, maybe [the reason I needed to share is] because I lost my joy for the game. I used to play sport for the joy. I loved being a member of a team and pushing myself to improve. It used to be my favorite part of the day, something I would look forward to from the minute one session was over until the next started. By the time I went through one season with you, I lost that joy. I was more relieved than distressed after my last competitive game ever. It was the sport I had loved for so long and played for eighteen years, and it was done, and I was relieved. How bad is that? By the end, I didn't even want to play anymore. Did you know it took me two years to even think about wanting to play again? I couldn't do it. I'm still working on trying to rediscover the joy that I lost.

Even the process of writing this letter has been distressing. I've noticed my core start to heat up. I feel angry. I feel sad. My body is tensing up. I'm irritated.

If there is one thing I do know, it's that I'm not writing this because I feel sorry for myself. I learned and grew through my time with you, which has nothing to do with you but everything to do with the fact that I am, and was before I ever met you, a mentally tough person. You could have harnessed that in a positive manner. You could have helped me use my own mental toughness to push myself to the next level. Instead of helping me use my inherent mental toughness to get better at the game, I found myself having to use it to endure you. Mental toughness isn't a limitless resource, "Coach," so since I was having to use a portion of mine on trying to overcome your ridiculous coaching tactics, I was only left with so much to use in our sport. I'm still learning and growing, but it was difficult. No, it was more than difficult; it was onerous. It's not something an athlete should have to go through.

So, what do I want to tell you? My hope is that you, too, are learning and you, too, are growing. I'm not writing this letter from a perfect place. Don't get it twisted. I know I am not a perfect person, but I am responsible enough to work on the things I need to improve, so I ask that you keep working on yours. Because you need it, and, more important, the athletes need and deserve it.

Letter 27: Reflection

What stood out to you in this athlete's letter?

_____

_____

_____

_____

_____

If you were the athlete in this situation, how would you react to the coach if you had experienced all these things? What would you do to express your concerns?

_____

_____

_____

_____

If you were the coach in this situation, how would you respond to the athlete if this letter were written to you? Consider your initial reaction as well as any behavioral changes you might make.

_____

_____

_____

_____

_____

LETTER 28

Dear Coach,

You wanted us to look like everyone else. We were not allowed to wear our hair the way we wanted to, which was ironic because you always seemed to turn a blind eye when the [high-profile] athletes dyed their hair [those crazy colors]. We couldn't let our jewelry show. We had to make sure our shirts were always tucked in, literally, at all hours of the day. I was told on multiple occasions that I should stop looking so "hippie" and dress a little more "professional"—whatever that was supposed to mean. Tattoos, well, you never really spoke explicitly against them by saying we couldn't have them, but I remember sitting around with some of my [teammates] when I heard you call one of the players a "gay-[person]" because of the new tat they got a few days prior. I remember feeling shamed because, little did you know, I had several tattoos. They just weren't visible. You didn't even care to ask them (or anyone else for that matter) the meaning behind their tattoo. If you would have asked, maybe you would have learned [my teammate's] tattoo was actually something they got on their arm to keep their head in the game so they could perform better.

When I first started playing for [this organization], I willingly followed the rules. I mean, I was given this opportunity to play here. I remember being told that I should stop complaining and just be proud to wear the [organization's logo] on my chest. In those first years, I just lowered my head and did it because it's what had to be done if I wanted to move [to the next level]. What I really learned, though, was to hide myself. Year after year, I lost a little bit of who I was. The "hippie" in me? Yeah. That was inspired by my [parent] who had died a few years back. It was my way of honoring them, keeping them alive. Did you know that when you told me I should stop being so "hippie" and dress more "professional," what I heard you say was, "Your [parent's] influence has no place here." Screw you for that.

I am not sure when and how everything I just said became the norm in [our sport]. I am not here to say that tradition doesn't have a time and place, but I do think that when tradition overshadows a person's authentic self, that's when we have a problem. I needed to express myself, Coach. I wanted to [wear my hair like that] because, this might seem silly to you, but it gave me more confidence, made me feel more like [an adult]. But because I had to wear my hair a certain way, it made me feel like a child. Probably because you were just another adult using your position of authority as a means to control us. It seems minor, I know. The way a person wears their hair shouldn't influence their sport performance, but you did always tell us that the "wins were won" because we paid attention to the small, fundamental details of the game. My hair, as an example, was a small detail that not only mattered to me but to a lot of my other teammates as well. If you wanted us to play like grown [adults], then you should've let us do what we needed to do to *feel* like grown [adults]. Maybe wearing your hair [that certain way], not having tattoos, and dressing more "professional" was your way of feeling and playing like [an adult] back in your prime, but please do not prescribe your way of living life onto the rest of us.

I really wish I would have caught on to this sooner instead of learning the lesson retrospectively. I wish I would have stood more proudly in my authenticity instead of letting you strip me of who I am based upon what you thought I should be to get to the next level. It's taken me a lot of years to get myself back, so I am writing this letter, not just for you but for other athletes who are experiencing the same thing. Hear this, athletes: be who you are. If your coach doesn't champion that, don't waste your life away trying to please someone who drank the juice and lost sight of their authenticity a long time ago. Who we are is more than sport.

Letter 28: Reflection

What stood out to you in this athlete's letter?

_____

_____

_____

_____

_____

If you were the athlete in this situation, how would you react to the coach if you had experienced all these things? What would you do to express your concerns?

_____

_____

_____

_____

If you were the coach in this situation, how would you respond to the athlete if this letter were written to you? Consider your initial reaction as well as any behavioral changes you might make.

_____

_____

_____

_____

LETTER 29

Dear Coach,

It all started when you made that comment while our team was eating dinner after a [competition]. You said, "Wow. I didn't expect you to finish that. You probably shouldn't be eating that much." I didn't think anything of it at the time. Looking back, though, I now know that's when it started: my eating disorder.

I didn't really understand eating disorder culture. I mean, I had heard about it, but I never expected to be a victim of it. I always had a healthy relationship with food. After going to therapy, I realized why I did it, though. I went to your program because of the funding you promised you'd provide me. I needed that funding in order to continue competing in [the sport] I loved so much. So, when you made the comment about how much I was eating, I subconsciously made the connection: I need to eat less in order to weigh less, which supposedly meant performing better. Subconsciously, I thought you were funding me to be there, so I felt I owed it to you to be the best "employee." I started restricting myself. I started to view food as the enemy. On some occasions, I binged. Then there were other seasons where I simply denied myself food.

I continued the cycle because, well, I was getting results. I weighed less; thus, I performed better—until I didn't. For the first year, my performance was the best it had ever been. You were praising me for my results, but what you didn't know is what I was doing to achieve those results. You might have thought you were only positively reinforcing my performance, but what you didn't know is that you were positively reinforcing my eating disorder as well. As long as you were happy, I kept doing what I needed to do. I binged. I restricted.

It was during the second year that things started to break down. An eating disorder usually catches up to you sooner or later. It took a year for me to start feeling the detriments of what I had put my body through and a year and a half for you to see it, too. My bones were fragile. My energy was low, which crushed my performances. You started to get frustrated and even made a comment about how I needed to start to eat more— how ironic considering what you used to say to me. Did you want me to eat more or eat less? That's when I started to lose my mind. I didn't know how to please you anymore.

Thankfully I am writing this letter in a healthier place now. I've processed what I needed to process, which allowed me to see things more realistically once I wasn't so close to the situation. Coach, I needed you to not just judge me based on my performance. Every little thing I did was obsessively observed through a performance lens. You watched what I ate and judged it based upon how it was going to influence my performance. You monitored our sleep schedules only because it mattered to how we performed. You had a say in who we hung out with, which meant heavily encouraging us not to have significant others because they were too distracting to our performance. But what I realize now is that you only cared about how we performed because of how it made you look. You used us for your personal gain.

This is what I wish I could've told you, but because I was blind to it at the time, I didn't say it then. I don't think you realize your power. You threw words around without any accountability to them. You might not think a measly comment about food was going to harm me in the way that it did, probably because you thought everyone sitting at the dinner table that night would have thought you were just joking as you laughed off your comment. What I learned through counseling is, Coach, that was abuse in disguise. You need to be more careful. I guess I could ask that you hold yourself more accountable to what you say, but if you don't have someone else holding you accountable, then I doubt you'll actually change.

It's an issue with the system. There were days I wanted to march into your office and demand you pay for all the therapy bills that had accumulated over the years because you did this, but I don't have hard evidence that you sparked my eating disorder, so nothing is going to hold up in "court" if I ever felt safe enough to bring it to the [organization's] attention. I guess this letter has morphed into me not just telling you what I needed from you but also asking organizations to wake up. Where's the quality control of coaches? How are we going to ensure the coaches don't, in an off-hand comment, physically and psychologically damage humans? Do we create policy, enforce mandatory continuing education, or require certification? I don't know the answers, but I think we need to start talking and doing something about it.

Letter 29: Reflection

What stood out to you in this athlete's letter?

_____

_____

_____

_____

If you were the athlete in this situation, how would you react to the coach if you had experienced all these things? What would you do to express your concerns?

_____

_____

_____

If you were the coach in this situation, how would you respond to the athlete if this letter were written to you? Consider your initial reaction as well as any behavioral changes you might make.

_____

_____

_____

_____

_____

PART III:
The Truth

Before heading into Part III, I need to address two things. First, while this section is entitled "The Truth," with a capital *T* for grammatical purposes, it's necessary to note what I actually mean. I consider this section to be "the truth" with a lowercase *t* to emphasize an overarching belief that I hold. That is, I do not believe what you are about to read is, in any way, the all-encompassing, all-consuming, only Truth. Instead, it is one of many truths. Just as each athlete featured in this book shared their respective truth, I now want to share mine.

Second, I want to congratulate you for getting to this point in the book. I think it would be disrespectful not to acknowledge how hard some of those letters were to read. I appreciate your perseverance in considering them. Despite how challenging it might have been, you leaned into the hard anyway. I hope you wrote in the margins and made copious notes in your journal as you read each letter. Whatever stood out to you and might have affirmed or inspired change in your coaching style, I champion it. Because, to be quite honest, I think the letters speak for themselves.

Now comes the hard part—at least for me. What you are about to read in this next section came to me after a full day of writing. I was exhausted. I had hit the wall. I was shoulder-deep in research that validated each athlete's story, but writer's block was at an all-time high. To help curb my frustration, I decided to hit the sauna. In that space, I meditated and just allowed the universe to tell me what I needed to do. That's when I had an epiphany, which called me to do the most vulnerable thing I can imagine doing in this book.

When the thought popped in my head, my chest immediately became heavy. My throat tightened, which was my sign. I knew this is what I needed to do. I needed to get out of my professor headspace, which was trying to rationalize the athletes' letters with statistical research evidence. Instead, I knew I needed to do what I was asking of the athletes—put myself on the same playing field as them—and let my own personal sport story speak for itself. Thus, what you are about to read is a composite letter[11] I wrote before I started gathering the letters for this book. It is what I always wish I could have told my coach but, for whatever reason, never did.

LETTER 30

Dear Coach,

I needed you to take your hands off my neck, both physically and metaphorically. When I called, I needed you to pick up or at least call me back and follow up. What I wish you would have done is hear and believe what I was trying to tell you. I needed you to see the tap dance I was doing for you. It was a full show where I was wearing all the bells and whistles, but you always found a way to look past me, as if you were on a search for something more interesting. The funny thing is, what you were searching for was right in front of you: me.

You told me to be "coachable," though, so I listened to you. I did as you said, so I spent years doing that dance number, and as each year passed, I tapped louder to the beat of your drum. I thought I was doing it to please you, but the reality was, I did it to mute myself. I learned to hate myself because I thought you hated me by the subtle ways you would ignore me if we didn't win or by how much you would scold me if I didn't perform up to standard. Interestingly, I still cannot articulate your standard because I'm still unsure of what it was.

As time passed, I became more afraid of you. Why? Because every time I would approach you with a concern or an idea, you would shut it down and demand I trust you, which I always found perplexing. I did trust you. When I approached you to talk about various training schedules that either worked or didn't for my body, for instance, I wasn't doing so out of lack of trust in your coaching. Instead, I was doing it simply to provide you feedback. Maybe I wasn't articulating that well, or perhaps not as well as I am here in this letter, but I wish you would have understood that I was morphing into a young adult then. It was inevitable that I was going to stumble over my words and maybe not present my argument so well. That's a part of the whole learning process of life. What I needed from you then was to put your ego aside, not take my suggestions so personally, and realize I had the best for both of us in mind. Because what would have been best for me (i.e., a training schedule that challenged rather than broke my body) would have been best for you as well. I would have performed better and, thus, made you look good when I was standing on the "podium." But that never happened because you never listened to me.

Because you shut me down, I learned the only safe space for me was talking to the assistant coach, which turned our team culture into that of a dysfunctional family. For instance, after you threw that chair at us in the locker room, we knew we couldn't approach you about it. So, we went to the assistant coach, who eventually became the enabler of your abuse. At the time, I didn't realize it. Now, it makes sense. The assistant coach did whatever they knew to maintain peace. Thus, they tried to alleviate everyone's discomfort by telling us whatever they felt we needed to hear to make us feel better:

"I know it's frustrating. That's just how Coach is, though."

"You need to learn to block out Coach. Use this as an opportunity to exercise your focus muscles. Then you'll be mentally stronger, which will make you a better athlete."

"It could be way worse. At least it's not as bad as some of the stories you've read in the news recently about coaches getting fired."

"Coach just has a lot going on right now, so try to see it from their point of view."

Reflecting on these interactions, I'm getting angry again. I knew the assistant coach was just trying to make us feel better. Still, now I realize why it never did alleviate my frustration: because I—my emotions, thoughts, and overall well-being—was being dismissed. What I learned through sport is that everything revolved around you. I was simply there to perform, like a puppet. You were the puppeteer who held all the power; thus, you groomed us to silence in order to maintain this dysfunctional culture, which placed you on an untouchable pedestal. Nevertheless, I wanted to be a "good" athlete, so I became quieter, which eventually led me to become more callused, cold, and angry. Consequently, I suffocated myself with my own frustrated inner voice.

I don't even know who she is anymore, the younger me. I think she liked to laugh, run, play, dance, read, and watch the stars, but I had to kill her. I had to give up all those things because, according to you, I needed to "make sacrifices" and "give my all" if I wanted to be successful. Thus, I spent years trying to hone my craft, which sometimes happened at two in the morning because I couldn't sleep, thinking about how I didn't want to let you or the team down. Development is all I could think about because you only mentioned our "areas for improvement" and never once commended us for our performances. Or, if you did, you only did it in passing as if it were just a formality. Thus, I learned that who I was in the moment was not good enough. You repeatedly beat that same drum, which reinforced I always had to strive for something bigger, better, faster, stronger. I became obsessed with the mentality of being a "good" athlete. I sold my soul to it, and this mindset eventually seeped into the fabric of my being.

Some might wonder, why is this bad? I am an accomplished young adult with a PhD and my first book deal all before the age of thirty, so shouldn't I be thankful? I initially was until the day after I graduated with my PhD. On the day I received the degree, I was on a high. When they introduced me to the world for the first time as Dr. Sara Marie Erdner, it was the proudest day of my life. I did it. I set the highest goal one can achieve in academia, and I accomplished it. For twenty-four hours, I was the Queen of the World. A day later, I was at rock bottom. Why? Because I climbed atop that mountain with the hope of finding fresh air, but I died when I reached the top because, all along, I thought I'd find *it* there.

To be honest, I don't even know what *it* was. Was it to find myself, the person in which I had lost touch? Maybe it was to find your approval, which morphed into diligently trying to find the admiration of others. I climbed tooth and nail to get to the top of that academic mountain of achievement. I finally got the approval of my four dissertation committee members, which solidified my stance in the world as a newly christened PhD. Even so, I suffocated atop that mountain because the oxygen I thought I was going to encounter ended up being the carbon dioxide of particular *others*.

I've since been in counseling to unpack my loneliness and depression, which I've learned is tethered to this sense of feeling like an *outsider*. Thus, I've worked diligently my whole life to gain *inside* access. Because of how you socialized me into sport, I was treated more as a commodity than a person. I then started to interact with myself in such a way as to fit my perfectly athletic, "square" self into the round hole that we call sport. If I had one more chance to sit across from you, this is what I would ask: What does it mean to be a "good" athlete, a "successful" athlete? I don't think we ever discussed that, which left it up to me—a young kid—to define it by how I experienced it. What you should know is this: How I experienced sport wasn't just influenced by you but also by the sociocultural narratives that clouded my mind as I participated. While we can't change what happened between us, I want to share with you what I wish I would have told you then.

I'm not saying winning shouldn't matter, but how you pursued it needed to change if you wanted to experience higher levels of performance from me. You would have gotten more out of me as an athlete if you understood me as a person in context. That is, when I played for you, I wasn't just an athlete. At the time, I identified as an adolescent, cisgender, heterosexual, Christian, female raised in the South by a middle-class, heterosexual, nondivorced family. What I learned through my education was that my identity was not the same as those who built sport. That is, young males wrote the story of sport; thus, the definitions of "sport excellence," historically speaking, and in which you held me accountable, were created by and for wealthy, young, able-bodied, Caucasian males.[12] Because you mindlessly coached, you never stopped to realize you were coaching my female body to conform to the prevailing culture of sport: an institution created by men for men to produce "better" men.

That's when I understood my loneliness and depression more deeply. It wasn't just because I felt like an outsider, from a macro-level perspective: being a female in a male-dominated world. My loneliness and depression were caused by a deeper underlying problem: The disconnection that ensued between us because you only acted kindly toward the aspects of me that fit the standards of what it means to be a "man." In contrast, you often behaved coldly toward the features that you deemed "needed some work," which I can't help but assume is because you didn't think they were "man" enough.

For instance, at the crossroads of my female and Christian demographic, you would have found a societal narrative that didn't champion "aggression on the [playing field]," which you always preached. At the time, I was a god-fearing woman who, according to what I learned in church about how to be a "good woman," was supposed to be meek and mild. So, when you blindly asked me to "be more aggressive"[13]—a phrase we often glorify in sport to uphold a fragile male identity[14]—you did so without consideration for *all* the macro-level forces that subconsciously pulled on me.

On the one hand, I was an athlete. I was supposed to be, according to you, aggressive, intimidating, strong, and a leader. On the other hand, I was—and still am—a cisgender, heterosexual, female. I was—and still am—expected by society to operate in this world with utmost grace, kindness, understanding, submissiveness, and overall pristine goodness.[15] Picture it, Mother Teresa wearing an athletic uniform. The two lists mentioned above are in direct opposition to one another. You might imagine then the cognitive dissonance my athletic identity created when stacked against the intersectionality of my cisgender, heterosexual, female identity.

None of the above mentioned insinuates that I'm not cut out for sport. You knew I was a phenomenal athlete, but your frustration got the best of you. Why? Because the way you defined being a "good" and "successful" athlete didn't align with how I expressed it. I was an aggressive, intimidating, strong leader. I still am. But, because I didn't express those characteristics the same way you did, you ignored me altogether. Just because my way and your way didn't conceptually and operationally look the same, doesn't mean either is wrong. Instead, it just means they are different. All roads lead to Rome.

After I retired from sport and started my higher education journey is when I learned how detrimental it is for various coaching methods not to consider and champion *all* athlete sociocultural demographics. I reflect upon one of [my teammates]; how they felt trying to navigate their gay identity amidst your overt and covert homophobic comments? I remember my [LatinX teammate] who played amongst a team of all Caucasians. Did they feel safe? I question whether [one of my teammates] felt seen and heard as they tried to navigate practice and games after hearing the news of their parent's divorce. What about my [teammate] who identified as an atheist? I cannot imagine how they felt each time you required us to hold a Christian prayer before all practices and games. How did that make them feel? I remember being frustrated for all of them when they mentioned their disdain for your lack of acknowledgment & subsequent compassion regarding their respective situations and identities.

It's imperative I also mention this: Not all people who identify as female experience female-ness in the same way. Just like, for example, how not all people who identify as a different race, sexual orientation, or religious affiliation experience those various identities the same. So, how I might conceptualize a "good" and "successful" athlete, will not always align with the individual who holds the same or different identities as me. In this sense, I needed you to consult my thoughts and champion my reality, which is what you should have done for each of my teammates as well.

Because you adopted and imposed how we've generationally defined a "good" and "successful" athlete upon me, this is what I came to perceive: a "good" athlete is a quiet athlete, and to be successful, I needed to unquestioningly follow your lead, which you often called "being coachable." In this sense, I learned to live my life by asking WWCD: what would Coach do? Instead, you should have empowered me also to ask, WWSD: what would Sara do? Because you groomed me to chase your validation, and your validation only, I lost my agency—and not just in sport. I carried this deferential mindset into other realms of my life: school, home, social life. Thus, what you gifted me is this: a voice in my head that was not my own.

What I needed instead was for you to empower my voice, which is an aspect permanently intertwined with my sociocultural factors. Thus, I didn't need you to tell me to find a way to separate my female-ness from my athlete-ness. Instead, I needed you to help me find a way to create synergy between them. I needed you to champion me as a human first. Specifically, I needed you to understand my worth should be fueled by my sense of self rather than solely from your biased perspective.

Through my education, I learned that optimal performance only happens when you create a safe environment for both of us. Because of your position of power, and because of how the system is built, you had the privilege to create an environment that best suited you and solely made you feel most comfortable. Because I didn't know any better at the time, I unquestionably morphed into it. However, what I realize now is that for me to feel safe, I needed you to inquire *and* care about my story. Then, I needed you to create a space that unconditionally honored *all* my identities, no matter if my identities aligned with the dominant storyline glorified in sport: an often sexist, homophobic,[16] and racist[17] narrative. What I just asked of you to do for me, I beg of you to do for others as well.

Sincerely,

Sara

Letter 30: Reflection

What stood out to you in my letter?

_____

_____

_____

_____

_____

If you were me, how would you react to the coach if you had experienced all these things? What would you do to express your concerns?

_____

_____

_____

_____

If you were my coach in this situation, how would you respond if this letter were written to you? Consider your initial reaction as well as any behavioral changes you might make.

_____

_____

_____

_____

_____

_____

I have to admit that as I was rereading my letter and making the vulnerable decision to share it with you all, I felt so much empathy for you, the coach. Through my education, I realized the problem is much bigger than coaches. You are likely a casualty, too; you are a product of the system: likely an athlete who turned into a coach. Whoever hired you probably did so solely based on your previous athletic and coaching experiences, so you did what came naturally to you. You treated us how your former coaches treated you.[18] Essentially, you didn't know better because no one likely championed you to learn better, so I started to feel the pain *with* you. I am not wagging my finger *at* you; instead, I am saying, no one is immune to spreading unhealthy patterns. We were all subjected to a system that advocated for this *win-at-all-costs* culture. Maybe you are lucky enough to be like the athletes in Part I who had a positive experience and were able to write a thank-you letter to their coach. Or maybe you had mediating agents in your life—parents, teachers, mentors—who offered you a healthier way of operating in the world and tempered the effects of athletics. However, I don't think we should leave it up to luck when considering the development of young minds. Thus, I want to invite you, Coach, to write your own Dear Coach letter.

Take some time to consider a former (or maybe even current) coach to whom you would like to write your letter. It doesn't matter which coach you choose. They can be at the youth, club, college, professional, or Olympic level. You can write either a thank-you letter, a not-so-good letter, or both. It doesn't matter how long ago the person coached you, and I set no page limits or word counts. I just ask that you not hold back as you address the following question: *What do I wish I could have told my coach but, for whatever reason, never did?*

As you write, I encourage you not only to think about what you liked or disliked but also consider how your coach's behaviors influenced your thoughts, emotions, and, subsequently, your sport performance. If you note things you didn't like, write what you wish they would have done instead. I've given you some space below to write your letter; however, I encourage you to take this to your nearest journal if you either run out of space or prefer not to write in your books.

Dear Coach [insert name],

_____

_____

_____

_____

_____

_____

_____

_____

_____

_____

_____

_____

_____

_____

_____

_____

_____

_____

_____

_____

_____

Reread your letter. Are you digging deeply into your memories and gut feelings? Are you being completely honest? If you listed behaviors you liked or disliked, ask yourself: Why did I like or dislike that behavior? How did it influence my mental performance in sport *and* overall mental health in life? In what ways did it affect my physical sport performance? If you haven't already, go ahead and write down why you felt the way you felt.

Now, with your completed letter in hand, I invite you to read your letter as if it were written to you by one of your current athletes. That is, did you write of behaviors or attitudes in your former coach that are similar to what an athlete under your current care might write about you? During this reread, I welcome you to highlight, circle, or underline your former coach's behaviors, whether good or bad. Ask yourself, "Am I mimicking these behaviors today?" You may discover you are repeating actions that you dislike about your former coach. Or, you might circle a behavior you liked that you want to integrate into your own coaching. If you are not currently coaching, I invite you to consider how those under your immediate care (e.g., employees, children) might write about how you operate in other areas of your life (e.g., work, home). Before you begin this step, though, I want to acknowledge that rereading your letter with an inward focus is a vulnerable thing to do; thus, I ask you to take as much time as you need.

After you have reread the letter and made your various notes, make a list of what behaviors you believe you should

Continue doing _____

Stop doing _____

Start doing _____

I want to commend you for leaning into these exercises. As one of the athletes who wrote a letter for this book mentioned in an email exchange with me, "I thought it would be easy to write my letter, but that wasn't the case. It was hard, exhausting at times, to revisit those stories, which made me realize how much we need this: our stories will hopefully encourage effective change." The same holds true for you. Your letter, whether good or bad, is just as important.

Thus, you might be wondering, *What now? How do I take what I've learned in this book and put it into action?* If you feel compelled to share the insights with your athletes that you've encountered from writing your own Dear Coach letter or in reading and reflecting upon the athletes' letters offered in this book, I encourage you to do so. I simply ask that you approach the athletes with a spirit of empathy and compassion, not one that is attacking and blaming them for your choice of behaviors.

Here are three options for what this might look like in practice:

Option 1: Hold a team meeting. Articulate to the athletes what you've learned about yourself as a coach after reading this book. Possibly list out what you believe you should continue, stop, and start doing. Then, ask for their feedback. Do they concur or disagree with your insights? Would they, from their perspective, add, edit, or revise anything on your list? Remember, given the barrier of communication that historically has been prevalent within the coach-athlete relationship, it's likely that athletes might not be fully vulnerable and want to have open dialogue with you about the list you've shared. However, you must let them know it's an option—that you humbly are open to receive their constructive criticisms and subsequently use their suggestions to improve your coaching.

Option 2: Write each athlete on your team a letter articulating to them, in whatever fashion you see fit, what you've learned about yourself as a coach after reading this book. List various things in which you are proud. Apologize for any coaching behaviors you enacted upon them that you feel harmed them in any way. Make a note of how you plan to do better by not only them but yourself as their coach. At the end of the letter, encourage each athlete to write you a letter back, if they want to, addressing what they wish they could have told you but, for whatever reason, have not yet. If both you and the athlete are willing, continue having back and forth dialogue via letter exchange or possibly face to face. I simply suggest letting the athlete dictate the mode of communication.

Option 3: Identify the athlete(s) in which you believe you lack quality communication. Either in written form or face to face, apologize for whatever you feel needs forgiveness. Address the positives you see in that particular athlete, and then make it a point to overtly acknowledge the positives in not only that athlete but all members of the team moving forward. Note: for any of the options listed, if you want more support in considering how these various options might operate for your particular team, please contact me at doc.serdner.dearcoach@gmail.com.

While the options mentioned above are simply a few suggestions for how to implement an action plan at the micro-level, it's also imperative that we address the macro-level forces. As we've seen, the personal and emotional impact of coaches in an athlete's life is profound. But what about the forces that act upon you? As one athlete mentioned in their letter, "It's an issue with the system." As I read through each letter, it's clear to see that your role is complex, which causes there to be a higher probability that mental, emotional, and, quite possibly, physical chaos will ensue. You're doing your best to keep your head above water with all these hats you're supposed to wear, which get heavy. The weight of these various roles takes its toll, which begins to trickle down and detrimentally influences athletes. What we see here is this: You have the ultimate power to create a culture that not only operates within but also outside the lines of sport. However, I cannot help but think about how you must feel. Do you want to make the various changes that align with best coaching practices but feel that a higher power is tying your hands behind your back? Maybe then it's not just a Dear Coach letter we need to write but a letter to sport. Here's mine.

Dear Sport,

This letter is for all the sport administrators who have a powerful hand in how sport operates at the macro-level. I am writing this letter to ask that you untie both athletes' and coaches' hands from behind our backs, which starts by ceasing to fool yourself in thinking that "sport builds character."

You always like to say that, by default: "sport builds character." However, are you aware of history's mark upon this phrase? Namely, at the turn of the 20th century, this phrase was introduced in sport as a way to "tame what [authority figures] perceived as the savage, undisciplined character of younger, lower-class males from Irish and southern European immigrant families. Their intent was the create obedient citizens and productive workers."[19] So, when you continue to say "sport builds character," you're ultimately holding both athletes *and* coaches who hold various identities accountable to a phrase that's been applied primarily to males as a way to socialize them into being a "good man." Thus, it begs the question: Does sport actually build character, or does it just subject and then reduce all people to fit into the "good, productive man" mold?

What's missing is proper, fully informed, mandated coaching education where coaches can learn to use more mindful coaching pedagogies that promote inclusive integrity. Currently, your system allows athletes to become coaches based solely on technical and tactical intellect and/or previous athletic accomplishments. Thus, the voice in athletes' heads is molded by coaches whose inner dialogue is contaminated by their former coaches or other socializing agents who, often implicitly, thrust a sexist, homophobic, and racist narrative forward. This system ultimately promotes a culture that leads to a higher population of athletes writing not-so-good Dear Coach letters.

While mandating coaching education at all levels of play is necessary, it shouldn't stop there. There's a cyclical problem here, and I believe you notice it, too. I see the work you've done to try and resolve it. You have witnessed athletes struggling, and you've answered by creating various athlete mental health initiatives. While these initiatives are well-intended, necessary, and wonderful, we are only addressing half the problem, which leads me to ask: Have you considered how these initiatives possibly serve as a buffer to help athletes cope with abusive coaching? What about the coach? If there is one thing I learned through my athletic experience, as well as encountered in my research, it is this: coaches matter. They not only matter in and of themselves, but they also matter because of their profound influence on athlete well-being and overall sport performance.

How many athletes' mental health is in jeopardy at the hands of their coach? I know mine was along with a vast majority of athletes, as can be concluded from several of the letters offered in this book. So, while athlete mental health initiatives are great—something I wholeheartedly champion—I think you are putting all your money into a Band-Aid solution. Instead, I suggest a solution that might approach a cure: coach mental health initiatives.

I created this book because this is what coaches wanted; they craved to know what athletes thought about how they were doing. The athletes' letters in this book uncover some hard truths. During the two years I spent writing this book, I spoke to various coaches about its development. When I mentioned what I concluded in the last paragraph—we need coach mental health initiatives—I watched tears fill the eyes of some.

The idea that coaches sacrifice their own mental health resonated. They are drowning, losing precious time with family, and sacrificing time to nurture a genuine connection with players. Their giving, helping role makes them stressed out and exhausted, with no one to turn to for support. When their world gets chaotic, where is their encourager, their cheerleader? When the pressure to win gets so unbearable, who do they have to talk to? I think the honorable thing to do here is to support them, and I am not just talking about turning to their significant others or chatting with fellow coaches. I am talking about actual, financially funded access to mental performance *and* clinical counseling services.

Similar to how you expect athletes to build mental strength to gain the winning edge, why are you not encouraging coaches to do the same? They are performers, too. Coaches' thoughts, behaviors, and emotions influence how they perform their job in practice and on game days, which trickles down and subsequently influences athlete mental functioning. Thus, if you want athletes to be mentally strong, you must encourage coaches to seek guidance from certified mental performance consultants.[20] In those mental performance sessions, coaches can better learn how to let their minds can work *for* them rather than *against* them during practices and competitions, helping them take their mental game from good to great.[21]

In a similar vein, you often offer clinical counseling services for athletes. Why are the same services not available to coaches? As opposed to mental performance consulting, which helps coaches understand how to optimize their minds within sport, coaches also need space to navigate life's bigger concerns. In therapy, they can begin to unpack their personal anxieties and fears evoked by their lives outside of sport. This practice will allow coaches to better navigate their personal lives within the context of the counselor and coach relationship, which will help to maintain the sanctity of other relationships within sport. That is, coaches will be less likely to spill their grievances onto their loved ones, perpetuate the problem by complaining amongst their colleagues, or continue to take their frustrations out on the athletes. By providing coaches with both mental performance *and* clinical counseling services, this will allow coaches to model healthier behavior for athletes.[22]

You might question such a costly approach. But in reality, it's you, Sport, who put them in this position in the first place. The stress of performing, of proving themselves, is what undermines their health as a spiritual, emotional, and social being. You might not have verbally stated it, but I assume that at some point you called them into your office and emphasized their win/loss record. Coaches are aware that you hired them solely based upon their ability to produce wins on the scoreboard; thus, you have the power subsequently to fire them if they don't produce. Across generations, this pressure, no matter how influenced by it each coach might feel, has clouded their judgment. Maybe the coach started strong by wanting to develop athletes holistically.[23] Still, as the season progressed and you started breathing down their neck, prioritizing their win/loss record, they began to choke.

It's similar to how athletes choke during sport performance. During pressurized situations, athletes are more likely to choke if they fear negative evaluation.[24] I believe the same holds true for coaches because they fear they might lose their job if they do not produce wins. As the pressure rises, coaches choke. They change, even if only slightly, how they coach. Why? Because you have made winning the target, which, according to Viktor Frankl, is the last thing we should do:

The more you aim at [winning] and make it a target, the more you are going to miss it. For success, like happiness, cannot be pursued; it must ensue, and it only does so as the unintended side effect of one's dedication to a cause greater than oneself or as a by-product of one's surrender to a person other than oneself.[25] To sum up Frankl's quote in modern-day coaching terms: Your target shouldn't be winning. Your target should be the emotional, mental, and physical well-being of both coaches *and* athletes. Then, and only then, will winning ensue.

For years I was mad at my coaches, but fortunately, I came to realize it's not their fault. It wasn't the coaches' hands around my neck. It was yours. You were suffocating all of us with the mantra that "sports build character," and the only way to build it was to adopt a *win-at-all-cost* mentality, which you covertly championed. You never stepped in to renounce this attitude when it reared its nasty head. The underbelly of this approach is seen in yelling, demeaning, getting in athletes' faces, throwing things, and calling them names.[26] Yet we've accepted these coaching behaviors with the belief that they motivate athletes. We've willingly accepted, dare I say it, *abuse* at the hands of coaches because somewhere along the way someone decided that abusive coaching strategies produce optimal athletes. While it might seem like it helps in the short-term by evoking fear in athletes to mobilize them to meet the coaches' demands, it has long-term, detrimental effects. When I pause to reflect, I ask myself, *Who started the lie that negligence and maltreatment are okay—even preferable—in sport?*

Now, I know you might be thinking I'm being a little harsh. Abuse? Negligence? Maltreatment? Yes. We need to start recognizing this behavior for what it is. We often sugarcoat things to lighten the blow, especially if we performed that behavior ourselves or don't want to admit the pain it caused us. Thus, we take jabs at people, and then, when they don't find it funny, we shame them for not having a sense of humor. That's abuse in disguise. When we don't take the time to consider what we say, how we say it, and the effect it could have, that is negligence. When we throw things in the locker room out of frustration or get so close to someone's face as to violate their personal space, that is maltreatment. In any of the scenarios mentioned above—and I'm only naming a few—where is the consideration for human decency? Where is the respect for the other's emotional, mental, and physical space? We often don't ask ourselves these questions because, well, we have enabled the need for such behaviors by telling ourselves this is how it ought to be; this is sport.

In my Methods of Coaching course I teach at Adams State University, a few students respectfully challenged my stance on coach abuse, negligence, and maltreatment. One or two of the students played devil's advocate and said, "Well, I need that. I need the coach to get in my face and yell at me. It motivates me." I respectfully received their comments and, after a short pause, proceeded to very aggressively flip tables, throw my textbook up against the whiteboard, and loudly yell profane language into a couple of the students' faces: "I'm disappointed in you for not making an *A* on the last assignment. You're a disgrace to this class, so get out!"[27]

After I concluded my demonstration, the students all sat wide-eyed and completely silent, probably because they were not expecting that from me. I'm a petite, 5'5" professor who is usually in a joyful mood. Red-faced yelling and swearing is out of character for me. So, as they sat silently, and after I composed myself and apologized profusely, I told them this: If I came into this classroom every time we met—or even just a few times—and did what I just did, someone likely would go to my department chair and complain about me. I would have horrible end-of-the-course reviews, and give or take a semester—or maybe by the end of the week—I would be fired. Why? Because we do not tolerate that behavior in academia.

If I continued that abusive performance day-in and day-out in the classroom, those students—those who said that getting yelled at motivated them—probably wouldn't be motivated to make better grades. They would stop coming to class, likely lose respect for me, and undoubtedly demand a better professor. I wouldn't blame them. People do not deserve that kind of behavior in academia or any other realm of life, so why are we accepting it in sport? Why are we not demanding better?[28] I think it is because we never took off our hegemonic, rose-colored glasses. So, after generations of athletes and coaches experiencing such behavior, and in order to cope with it, they convinced themselves they needed such behavior to achieve optimal performance gains. Because we've placed winning as the target, we've unquestionably let this coping mechanism seep into the very fabric of all sport stakeholders' beings to the point that, when this behavior knocks, we open the door and warmly welcome abuse.

So, what I need from you, Sport, and what I believe both athletes and coaches need, is a safer environment that nurtures our mental performance *and* mental health in sport and life, which subsequently will enhance our physical performance. However, here's the thing: Coaches will not be able to give athletes what they need if coaches don't first experience it. Coaches are humans, too, who represent a wide array of various sociocultural identities that also deserve to be championed. Thus, it is necessary to understand the very foundation from which sport was built to understand better how to eradicate certain traditions that covertly marginalize those who don't fit into the wealthy, young, able-bodied, Caucasian male box. Even for those who find themselves categorized in that box, the societal narratives that define what it means to be a "good man" robs them of the chance to choose the kind of man they want to be.[29] In this sense, I am asking you to nurture our human souls by interacting with both coaches *and* athletes in an inductive rather than deductive manner: make sport fit the person instead of making the person fit sport.

Sincerely,

Sara

Now, while those were just some of my truths, I'm curious to know what you'd like to say to the system? I want to encourage you to write a Dear Sport letter. You can keep it general, addressing it solely to "Sport," or you can think about a particular sport administrator within your respective organization to whom you'd like to direct the letter. In this particular letter, I invite you to consider what changes you believe the organization needs to make for sport to be a safe environment not only for the athletes but also for you. I invite you, when thinking about what you want to include in the letter, to consider how the athletes' letters in this book have inspired you to make changes. How might your own Dear Coach letter influence the changes you think need to be made at the systemic level? How might the various attitudes and/or expectations set forth by your administration impede the changes you want to make? On the flip side, how might your administration already champion your positive evolution as a coach? If you identify with the latter, I encourage you to write them thank-you letters. There are no page limits or word counts. I just ask that you not hold back as you address the following question: *What do you wish you could tell your sport administration but, for whatever reason, have not yet?*

As you write, I encourage you to write about the things you appreciate and/or the things that need to change. How do these things, both the good and bad, influence your thoughts, emotions, and, subsequently, your mental and physical performance as a coach? If you note things you didn't like, write what you wish the administration would do instead to support you and the athletes. I've given you some space below to write your letter; however, I highly encourage you to use a journal if you run out of space or prefer not to write in your books. Be sure to write with a humble, empathic tone so that your observations may be well-received—the same tone I hope you've experienced from the athletes' letters written in this book.

Dear Sport [or insert the administrator's name],

_____

_____

_____

_____

_____

_____

_____

_____

_____

_____

_____

_____

_____

_____

_____

_____

_____

_____

_____

_____

_____

Whether you decide to give this letter to one of your administrators or not, I hope these activities, along with the letters in this book, have encouraged you not only to hear athletes' voices but also to realize how important it is for us to listen to yours. Because, as a collective, what we need to understand is this: no one coaches in a vacuum. Your coaching is influenced by your past, which seeps into the present and contaminates the future of sport. I've spoken to many coaches who, when asked why they coach as they do, stated something similar to this quote:

It's because that's how I was coached, I guess. I remember Coach placing the white towel out in the field and telling us that was the target, that's what we needed to aim for. That was thirty years ago. I've kept that drill alive today—did it as recently as two days ago because that's just what has been done. It's all I ever knew. Is it the best way of doing it? I don't know. I am not sure if there is another way, but when I talk to my coaching buddies, no one suggests anything else.

This quote hints at the solution we need. We live in an echo chamber where we've stayed within the confines of the system: coaches teaching coaches, administrators mentoring other athletic administrators, and athletes supporting athletes. As a scholar, I can tell you that academia has done the same. Namely, I have been a part of various conversations and research projects that explored "good" versus "bad" coaching, and its influence on athlete well-being and sport performance. While researchers have made strides in investigating athletes' perceptions of poor[30] and excellent coaching,[31] most research efforts get caught in the vacuum of research journal publications and academic conference presentations. That is, in our respective fields, university administrators praise professors for publishing research in prestigious journals, presenting our findings at various academic conferences, getting a pat on the back from our colleagues, and then moving on to the next research project. What's missing is the bridge between us, the academics, and coaches who work directly with athletes.

Within academia, just as in sport, the problem is systemic. Whether I receive tenure as an assistant professor usually is not evaluated on how well I disseminate my research to the general public. I am reviewed based upon my research productivity, service to the institution, and teaching. Thus, most scholars want to get their findings to you, but we do not have the time nor the resources to do so. Instead, we stay in our system, similar to how you stay in yours. This compounds the issue, though; if we do not go outside the system, we cannot truly learn how to inform coaching practices better or let coaching practices influence our research efforts.

Thus, while it is vital to speak with those within your system, the need for external consultation to determine if, for instance, that particular drill is the best tool to nurture success is crucial. The current dysfunction has been fueled by a siloed approach, which means the answers will likely come from a multisystem collaboration, such as a quality partnership between academia and athletics.

Thus, beyond just offering a micro-level action plan that coaches can implement immediately, it's also important to pose the following two-fold, macro-level question. What policies can we enact that (a) hold academics who study sport accountable to collaborate with and disseminate inclusive research to athletics and (b) require athletics to align their administrative and coaching practices with scientifically supported research? I pose this collaboration with full understanding that it's not without its limitations. That is, just as sport was created by and for the wealthy, young, able-bodied, Caucasian male, the academy was built on similar structures. As such, the academy, at large, often excludes the lived experiences of those who populate marginalized groups.[32] While that goes beyond the scope of this book, it's important to acknowledge this limitation to (a) encourage the academy to address this issue and (b) highlight the need for athletic administrators and coaches to use research that champions diverse voices—not just using research that examines a population of Caucasian males and then applying those findings to athletes and coaches who are not Caucasian males. In this way, we can slowly break down and thus integrate each of the silos in the system: academics, athletes, coaches, and athletic administrators.

From my perspective, the academy needs to reevaluate academic procedures. That is, it should be made a requirement for faculty and staff to be evaluated upon diversity and inclusion parameters within the tenure and promotion process and/or end-of-the-course merit reviews. Additionally, academics should be required to add more than just a paragraph or two of "practical application" to a research article. More is needed in this regard—because research articles aren't easily accessible to the general public—to bridge the gap between theory and practice. Similarly, how might athletic administrators ensure coaches are evaluated during the hiring, retention, and firing stages in such a way that aligns with scientifically supported, inclusive, best practices? Sport organizations would then be held accountable to a higher standard than just being able to make employment decisions vaguely based on a "good cultural fit."

In conclusion, we need to "wake up," as one athlete mentioned in their letter. We need better "quality control of coaches." We need to do everything we can "to ensure that coaches don't, in an off-hand comment, physically and/or psychologically damage" themselves and the "humans" under their care. This is our call to action:

We must empower and advocate for athlete voices because, for far too long, we have muted the very voices of those who can inform positive change in sport. However, we've also done a poor job at empowering and advocating for you, the coach, beyond helping you achieve wins. While I wrote this book to support athletes, I hope you feel that I wrote this book for you as well because you matter. You have always mattered. I am sorry if you have ever felt anything less.

These letters are only the beginning of what I hope to be an ongoing conversation. One that champions better initiatives to support both you *and* athletes with the hope of tearing down the communication barrier that currently stands in sport. Until these macro-level policy changes happen (mandated coaching education, mental health initiatives for coaches, and better collaboration between athletics and academics, which I've simply proposed as starting points), I hope this book inspires you to better empathize with athletes *and* yourself. When we begin by hearing and believing other peoples' stories *and* by respecting our own—because open and honest dialogue is the foundation of quality connection with ourselves and others—we can build higher quality coach-athlete relationships. And, it's necessary to note, this partnership should never be "an add-on to or by-product of the coaching process, nor is it based on the athlete's performance, age, gender [or other sociocultural factors]—instead it is the *foundation* of coaching." [33]

Winning then will only ensue when we place the development of the coach-athlete relationship at the forefront of best coaching practices, which, we must not forget, is intimately influenced by the interplay between both relational parties' sociocultural factors and the inherent power dynamics within the relationship. In this way, coaches will learn to interact with athletes by inclusively championing their various identities rather than overtly and covertly forcing athletes to fit into the fixed-conceptualization of what we've traditionally known sport to be.

Once sport respectfully acknowledges and mandates this philosophical shift, individuals and teams will "unambiguously reach a [higher] level of normative performance success,"[34] such as a world championship gold medal. Once this shift occurs, psychological growth will flourish and give way to a holistically healthier and safer sport environment for all. Thus, it's not about winning the game at all costs but rather about leaning into the vulnerability, empathy, and compassion needed to foster better communication so we can win the relationship.

ACKNOWLEDGMENTS

I could not have written this book without the courageous help of the athletes who shared their powerful letters. I am a better person because of knowing your stories, and I truly believe the world is a better place because you told them. I can only hope I did justice by you all. Inspired by your courage, I want to acknowledge all athletes. Even if this book doesn't fully capture your own story, please know that I hear you, believe you, and care. I call all coaches and other individuals who hold positions of power within athletics to do the same: hear the athletes you work with, believe them, and care about their stories.

I also want to thank the many coaches who have already challenged the status quo. I think I speak for all athletes when I say this: thank you for empathizing with us, empowering us, and being relationally vulnerable. To the coach who might be late to the relational party, no worries. That's why I wrote this book. Maybe before now, you were never permitted or did not know how to nurture the relational side of your job because, quite possibly, you weren't shown this same kind of care as an athlete. I appreciate you for picking up this book and starting your journey. Your athletes will thank you for it. I thank you for it. The world is a better place because of your openness.

To my mother, Cheryl Erdner. Even amidst our differences, which created challenges at times, you heard me, believed me, and cared about the story I wanted to write. Do you remember how adamant I was on career day in the fourth grade to dress up as an author? You enthusiastically dressed me in that god-awful white ruffled blouse and—as if the blouse wasn't enough to make my classmates bully me—you tucked it into my underwear to make sure it wouldn't come loose as I roughhoused on the playground. Thus, I was the kid with my shirt tucked into my underwear for extra support, which made it rise a little higher than my jeans. Looking back, I shouldn't be surprised because the extra support from my underwear was representative of your parenting style. You deserve all the roses, daisies, and rainbows for the countless hours of unconditional support you've given me throughout the years. You've danced along to the beat of my crazy drum, and for that, I am forever grateful.

To me academic community, thank you for not only teaching me the ways of qualitative research but for also encouraging me as I navigated the road less traveled:

To Dr. Jed Blanton, we didn't interact very much during my tenure at the University of Tennessee-Knoxville, but you still supported me by attending my dissertation defense. Immediately following, you sent a kind email encouraging me to take my "intense set of findings" and "share their narratives in a book." That email propelled me forward. It was probably a small act for you, but it was one of the more influential emails I've ever received.

To Dr. Dominic Morais, I kept waiting for the day you'd get fatigued by my endless phone calls and stop answering. I can't thank you enough for serving as a much-needed soundboard as I worked through how to articulate some of my hard truths. Your patience through my chaos kept me grounded. I confidently can say I am a better person because of our friendship.

I also want to thank the rest of my academic community for making this process feel less lonely: Drs. Rebecca Zakrajsek, Leslee Fisher, Lars Dzikus, Brian Gearity, Lauren Moret, Earlynn Lauer, Brian Zuleger, Johnsa Phares, and George McConnell. Because of you, I grew not only as a scholar but also as a human being. The world is a better place because all of you are in it.

To Bre, my niece, I look at you and see the future, which is what motivates me to make a positive change in this world. I can only hope that when you grow up, you and your entire generation will benefit from the work I am doing now. This book is my promise to fight for a better world.

To my publishing and editorial team, thank you for taking a chance on me, an unknown author with a passionate message. To David Hancock, thank you. I remember how nervous I was to pitch my book idea to you. The enthusiasm you showed me, though, was the match that kept this two-year writing extravaganza of a fire burning. I also would be remiss not to mention John O'Sullivan, CEO and Founder of Changing the Game Project. Thank you, John, for introducing me to David. I am forever grateful for your mentorship. You both have made my world and undoubtedly the worlds of others better because of the vision and mission you both promote.

To Amanda Rooker and your team of warrior editors, thank you. I began writing this book with immense insecurities, even after almost two decades of writing for academia (imposter syndrome is real, everyone). I love how you empathized, empowered, and were relationally vulnerable with me throughout the entire process. I also want to thank Lindsey Wente; your last-minute editorial help felt life-saving. I've truly grown as a writer and a human being from being in relation with you.

ABOUT THE AUTHOR

SARA ERDNER received her PhD in Sport Psychology and Motor Behavior from the University of Tennessee-Knoxville, where she also completed her Master of Science in Communication Studies, with an emphasis in interpersonal communication. She currently works as an assistant professor of coaching and coordinator of the Master of Science in Coaching (online) degree at Adams State University. As a Certified Mental Performance Consultant (CMPC®, #712) through the Association of Applied Sport Psychology (AASP), Sara also conducts independent mental performance services for a wide variety of performers, which includes working with youth, college, Olympic, and professional athletes.

As a scholar, Sara has been honored with two national research awards. In 2012, Sara received the top-paper award at the 98th Annual National Communication Association Convention. In 2017, she was awarded the Student-Athlete Development Research Award at the National Association of Academic Advisors for Athletics (N4A) Conference. Aside from her scholarly achievements, Sara has presented on the national and international stage, with her most notable appearances at Universität Tübingen in Germany; Jahrestagung der Arbeitsgemeinschaft für Sportpsychologie (German Sport Psychology Conference) at the University of Bern in Switzerland; at the United States Center for Coaching Excellence; and at various annual AASP conferences.

As an athlete, Sara has competed in many different sports. Growing up, she played softball, volleyball, and basketball. In college, Sara competed in a variety of triathlon competitions on the University of Tennessee TriVol Team. At the national level, Sara and her TriVol team of eleven other runners ran Ragnar, a 200-mile relay race from Chattanooga to Nashville, Tennessee, winning first place out of a total of 121 teams. Once she concluded her endurance sport tenure, due to a broken foot, she began to train and eventually placed first in her weight class in the Southeast Tennessee Strongman competition, moving a total of 11,300 pounds of weight in one day.

In her spare time, Sara is a proud artist who enjoys painting, playing her piano, and writing. Aside from the arts, she also likes living a spontaneous life, spending time outdoors, having philosophical conversations, traveling, climbing, skiing, cycling, camping, hiking, laughing, and cuddling with her rescue Husky/pit bull dog-hter, Kira.

ENDNOTES

1   C. R. Berger, "Beyond Initial Interaction: Uncertainty, Under-
    standing, and the Development of Interpersonal Relation-
    ships," in Language and Social Psychology, eds. H. Giles and
    R.N. St. Clair (Baltimore: University Park Press, 1979).

2   S. M. Erdner and C. N. Wright, "The Relationship between
    Family Communication Patterns and the Self-Efficacy of
    Student-Athletes," Communication & Sport 6, no. 3 (2018):
    368–389.

3   J. B. Miller, Toward a New Psychology of Women (Boston:
    Beacon Press, 1976).

4   According to relational-cultural theory, and in order to truly
    understand relationships, we must analyze and understand them
    within the larger cultural and societal contexts in which they
    occur. That is, in every relationship there are various socio-
    cultural aspects (e.g., race, gender, sexual orientation) that
    influence how people interact with others who are similar or
    different from them. Similarly, power dynamics within the rela-
    tionship also influence interpersonal dynamics. For example, as
    a coach, you might identify as a Caucasian male who overtly
    shares religious beliefs. While none of the aforementioned
    sociocultural factors are wrong (Caucasian, male, religious),
    it's imperative that coaches understand the socially constructed

narratives around such factors that might subconsciously influence the kind of relationship they have with particular athletes: the African-American athlete's relationship with a Caucasian coach. The female athlete's relationship with a male coach. The homosexual athlete's relationship with a coach that preaches against homosexuality because of their religious beliefs. All of these are instances, to name a few, that have the potential to impede relational growth. If you're curious to know more, please contact me at doc.serdner.dearcoach@gmail.com.

5 M. Sarkar and D. Fletcher, "Psychological Resilience in Sport Performers: A Review of Stressors and Protective Factors," Journal of Sports Sciences 32 (2014): 1419–1434.

6 D. Fletcher and M. Sarkar, "A Grounded Theory of Psychological Resilience in Olympic Champions," Psychology of Sport and Exercise 13 (2012): 669–678.

7 M. Sarkar, D. Fletcher, and D. J. Brown, "What Doesn't Kill Me . . . : Adversity Related Experiences Are Vital in the Development of Superior Olympic Performance," Journal of Science and Medicine in Sport 18 (2015): 475–479.

8 Sports included basketball, baseball, cross country and track/field, football, gymnastics, rowing, softball, soccer, swimming and diving, tennis, volleyball, and wrestling, to name a few.

9 Competition levels represented: high school, club, college, professional, Olympic.

10 Such as the names of the athlete and coach, sport, organizational affiliations, and technical and tactical terminology.

11 My composite Dear Coach letter is influenced by an autoethnographic technique, which infuses multiple storylines into one dramatic story with one composite character. I chose this method as a way to reinforce confidentiality. See C. Ellis, The Ethnographic I: A Methodological Novel about Autoethnography (Walnut Creek, California: AltaMira Press, 2004).

12 J. Coakley, "Studying the Past," In Sports in Society: Issues and Controversies (New York, New York: McGraw-Hill, 2007), 59.

13 Aggression is defined as "any behavior directed toward intentionally harming or injuring another living being who is motivated to avoid that harm." It is a physical and verbal behavior, not an attitude or emotion. While aggression is a complex concept, it's becoming all too common in sport, which reinforces the opportunities where it can be socially learned and subsequently adopted by athletes. That is, the behaviors modeled within the sport context by all stakeholders—coaches, administrators, fans, referees, parents—influence the kind of behaviors athletes will replicate. Therefore, authority figures within sport must mindfully encourage assertive (e.g., driving hard to the basket) as opposed to aggressive (e.g., purposefully embarrassing someone, saying something hurtful, making someone feel inadequate, trying to intimidate someone, or hitting another person). See R. S. Weinberg and D. Gould, "Aggression in Sport," In Foundations of Sport and Exercise Psychology (Champaign, Illinois: Human Kinetics, 2019), 567-583.

14 Sport was created by men for men as a call to overcome the direct threat women posed as they gained agency in society. What was called the "crisis of masculinity" (Kimmel, 1987), sport became a platform that acted as a "primary masculinity-validating experience" (Dubbert, 1979). Thus, sport became an arena that allowed white, middle-, upper-class males to create (a) separation from the supposed "feminization" of society and (b) reinforced the assumed natural superiority of men over women (Messner, 1988). Because of its origins, this is what constitutes its fragility. Thus, as it pertains to gender, women constantly are trying to navigate

their athletic identities as they maneuver through a world built by and for men to reinforce the socially constructed notion of masculinity. See M. A. Messner, "When Bodies are Weapons: Masculinity and Violence in Sport," International Review of the Sociology of Sport 25, no. 3 (1990): 203-220; M. S. Kimmel, "Men's Response to Feminism at the Turn of the Century," Gender and Society 1, no. 3 (1987): 261-283; J. L. Dubbert, A Man's Place: Masculinity in Transition (Englewood Cliffs, New Jersey: Prentice Hall, 1979), 164; M. A. Messner, "Sports and Male Domination: The Female Athlete as Contested Ideological Terrain," Sociology of Sport Journal 5, no. 3 (1988): 197-211.

15 J. Coakley, "Studying the Past," In Sports in Society: Issues and Controversies (New York, New York: McGraw-Hill, 2007), 63.

16 W. Lee and G. B. Cunningham, "Gender, Sexism, Sexual Prejudice, and Identification with U.S. Football and Men's Figure Skating," Sex Roles 74, no. 9-10 (2016): 464-471; I. H. Meyers, "Prejudice, Social Stress, and Mental Health in Lesbian, Gay, and Bisexual Populations: Conceptual Issues and Research Evidence," Psychological Bulletin 129, no. 5 (2003): 674-697.

17 B. Carrington, "The Critical Sociology of Race and Sport: The First Fifty Years," Annual Review of Sociology 39, no. 1 (2013): 379-398; K. Hextrum, "Bigger, Faster, Stronger: How Racist and Sexist Ideologies Persist in College Sports," Gender and Education (2019): 1-19.

18 Looking at coaching through a subjective educational theory (Kelchtermans, 2009) lens, we can better understand how coaching practices to date largely are informed by coaches' personal system of knowledge and beliefs. Thus, coaches have learned how to effectively build their coaching practices as well as their coach-athlete relationships based upon what

comes easiest to them, which doesn't always align with best practices. This philosophic approach encourages a coaching-centered practice, which ignores the experiences of athletes and highlights the importance for hearing, believing, and championing athletes' voices. See G. Kelchtermans, "Who I Am in How I Teach Is the Message: Self-Understanding, Vulnerability, and Reflection," Advances in Research on Teaching 19 (2013): 379–401.

19 J. Coakley, "Studying the Past," In Sports in Society: Issues and Controversies (New York, New York: McGraw-Hill, 2007), 72.

20 Through the Association for Applied Sport Psychology, Certified Mental Performance Consultant (CMPCs) are individuals with a master's or doctoral degree in sport science, psychology, or a closely related field who have met specific course requirements and have completed an extensive, mentored applied experience. The disciplines included within the sport psychology field applicable to those holding the CMPC® designation include clinical psychology, educational psychology and clinical mental health counseling, social work, industrial-organizational psychology, and sport psychology from a sport science basis. A CMPC® may work with a wide variety of participants in sport and performance. These individuals have obtained objective validation of their expertise in helping clients develop and use mental, life, and self-regulatory skills to optimize performance, enjoyment, and/or personal development in sport or other domains (e.g., performing arts, military).

21 P. Olusoga, I. Maynard, J. Butt, and K. Hays, "Coaching Under Pressure: Mental Skills Training for Sport Coaches," Sport and Exercise Psychology Review 10, no. 3 (2014): 31-44.

22 Only as recently as 1992 did the world learn about mirror neurons, which is the neuron in our brains that "mirrors" the behaviors of others in which we are surrounded. Thus, it's not just an opinion to state that we should properly model various behaviors that align with best practices, it's scientifically supported. Given the inherent power dynamics present within the coach-athlete relationship, coaches hold responsibility in regard to performing the kind of behaviors that promote optimal well-being and performance that we would like to see our athletes replicate (i.e., being mentally, emotionally, and physically healthy). See M. Iacoboni, "Imitation, Empathy, and Mirror Neurons," Annual Review of Psychology 60 (2009): 653-670.

23 National Coaching Standard 1, United States Center for Coaching Excellence.

24 C. Mesagno, J. T. Harvey, and C. M. Janelle, "Fear of Negative Evaluation and Choking," Psychology of Sport and Exercise 13 (2011): 60–68.

25 V. Frankl, Man's Search for Meaning (Boston, Massachusetts: Beacon Press, 1946), 16–17.

26 Many athletes experience emotional abuse from their coaches. Ashley Stirling & Gretchen Kerr, some of the leading researchers of abuse in sport, explored this phenomenon by first interviewing athletes in order to empirically define emotional abuse in sport. Their research revealed emotionally abusive coaching behaviors to be three-fold: physical behavior (e.g., acts of aggression such as hitting or throwing things at either the athlete or in the presence of an athlete), verbal behavior (e.g., yelling, shouting, belittling the athlete, name calling, using degrading comments, or humiliating the athlete in front of others), and denial of attention and support (e.g., not making verbal or nonverbal contact with the athlete after a "poor" performance, expelling or excluding the athlete from

practice or games). See A. E. Stirling and G. A. Kerr, "Defining and Categorizing Emotional Abuse in Sport," European Journal of Sport Science 8, no. 4 (2008): 173-181.

27 Please note: that was not in my lesson plan for the day; no students were physically harmed in the process; and I followed up with the class regularly to let them know that if they were triggered by my behaviors, we have various support services on campus with which I would gladly connect them.

28 This lesson was inspired by Dr. Lars Dzikus, my University of Tennessee-Knoxville sociology of sport professor.

29 J. Y. Sexton, The Man They Wanted Me to Be: Toxic Masculinity and a Crisis of Our Own Making (Berkeley, California: Counterpoint Press, 2019); L. Plank, For the Love of Men: A New Vision for Mindful Masculinity (New York, New York: St. Martin's Press, 2019).

30 B. T. Gearity, "Poor Teaching by the Coach: A Phenomenological Description from Athletes' Experience of Poor Coaching," Physical Education & Sport Pedagogy 17, no. 1 (2012): 79–96.

31 A. J. Becker, "It's Not What They Do, It's How They Do It: Athlete Experiences of Great Coaching," International Journal of Sports Science & Coaching 4, no. 1 (2009): 93–119.

32 Groups such as Black, LatinX, Middle Eastern, Native American, and other races except Caucasian, female, gay, lesbian, bisexual, transgender, non-cisgender, questioning, intersex, asexual, physical and mentally disabled or chronically ill, low socioeconomic status, Jewish, Muslim, Hindu, atheists, agnostics, and other religious affiliations except Christian.

33 S. Jowett, "The Coach-Athlete Partnership," The Psychologist 18, no. 7 (2005): 412–415.

34 S. Jowett, "The Coach-Athlete Partnership," The Psychologist 18, no. 7 (2005): 412–415.

Printed in the USA
CPSIA information can be obtained
at www.ICGtesting.com
JSHW022331140824
68134JS00019B/1427

9 781631 952845